THE AIR FORCE

THE AIR FORCE

"Aim High ... Fly-Fight-Win"

JASON C. ENGLE

amber
BOOKS

Published by Amber Books Ltd
United House
North Road
London N7 9DP
United Kingdom
www.amberbooks.co.uk
Instagram: amberbooksltd
Facebook: amberbooks
Twitter: @amberbooks

ISBN: 978-1-83886-060-8

Project Editor: George Maudsley
Designer: Mark Batley
Picture Research: Terry Forshaw

Printed in China

Contents

The Modern Air Force

The United States Air Force (USAF) of today is one shaped by post-Cold War geopolitical realities. The collapse of the USSR and the end of the Cold War saw a general draw-down of American armed forces. Comparatively tighter defense budgets, shrinking numbers of flying squadrons, fewer operational missiles, and fewer Airmen required USAF leaders to think more strategically and adopt a leaner, qualitatively superior, and more flexible organization to maintain its strategic advantages over near-peer challengers, such as China and Russia.

As the USAF looked to the twenty-first century, concepts of "forward defense" and "forward presence" had to be reconceptualized to fit the international landscape better as well as its own strengths and limiting factors. From numerous studies conducted by a variety of Air Force entities came the strategic vision of "global engagement," which viewed air and space power as inter-dependent and that superiority in both realms was essential in defense of the US. There is a logical progression from "global engagement" to the most recent priorities laid out by the Secretary of the Air Force: the build-up of the US Space Force (USSF); the continued modernization of its weapons, aircraft, systems, and equipment, as well as its institutional culture; the development of strong leaders and families; and strengthening international alliances.

While airpower theorists have long pointed to space as the ultimate "high ground" (and the set-up of the Space Force would seem to attest to that continued belief), it has been the people here on earth—Airmen, military and civilian, their families, and America's partner nations—that have been the Air Force's most important assets and they will be the ones who will pilot it into the future.

LEFT:
421st Fighter Squadron trains with the F-35A Lightning II
Air Force F-35A Lightning II pilots of the 421st Fighter Squadron return to Nellis Air Force Base, Nevada after flying a sortie as a part of the large-scale Red Flag combat exercise. The 421st, one of the longest-flying F-16 Fighting Falcon squadrons, recently transitioned to the F-35 and this exercise was intended to provide those pilots with valuable experience in the new aircraft.

LEFT:

1st Lieutenant Matthew Sanders on sortie, Afghanistan

1st Lieutenant Matthew Sanders, a 421st Expeditionary Fighter Squadron (EFS) pilot, prepares for a combat sortie in an F-16 Fighting Falcon at Bagram Airfield, Afghanistan. Airmen assigned to the 421st EFS, known as the "Black Widows," are deployed from Hill Air Force Base, Utah in support of Operation Freedom's Sentinel (a continuation of the Global War on Terrorism) and NATO's Resolute Support missions. Their mascot is derived from the squadron flying P-61 Black Widows during World War II.

RIGHT:

1st Lieutenant Landon Ellis flies a T-6 Texan II

1st Lieutenant Landon Ellis, an 8th Flying Training Squadron pilot, flies his T-6 Texan II over Vance Air Force Base (AFB), Oklahoma, returning from a four-aircraft flying formation for the USAF Basic Military Training graduation at Lackland AFB, San Antonio.

LEFT:

Refueling during Joint Warrior exercise, Scotland

Major Michael Harrison flies a KC-135 Stratotanker over Scotland to refuel aircraft participating in exercise Joint Warrior 19-1. Joint Warrior is a biannual, UK-led 13-nation exercise and one of the largest NATO exercises in Europe.

TOP RIGHT:

Bomber Task Force mission, Sweden

B-1s from the 28th Bomb Wing, Ellsworth Air Force Base, South Dakota integrate with Swedish Armed Forces Saab JAS 39 Gripens for the first time during a long-range, long-duration Bomber Task Force mission. Operations and exercises with allied and partner nations demonstrate a shared commitment to global security and stability and are among the Air Force's top priorities.

BOTTOM RIGHT:

B-1s return from a training mission in East China Sea

Senior Airman Jae Sajonas of the 9th Bomb Squadron helps align an MB-2 Tow Tractor on the flightline at Andersen Air Force Base, Guam. The 9th Bomb Squadron is a part of the 7th Bomb Wing, which deployed approximately 200 Airmen and four B-1s to support Pacific Air Force's (PACAF) joint force training efforts and strategic deterrence missions with allied and partner nations.

Pre-flight checks before Bomber Task Force mission to Nordic region
An aviator assigned to the 34th Bomb Squadron, Ellsworth Air Force Base, South Dakota, conducts pre-flight checks on a B-1B Lancer before takeoff in support of a Bomber Task Force (BTF) mission to US European Command (EUCOM). BTF missions reflect the US commitment to NATO and its allies to ensure their collective security.

LEFT:

C-17 Globemaster III maintenance

Air Force Senior Airman Zachary Anderson checks the tire pressure on a C-17 Globemaster III at the Pittsburgh International Airport Air Reserve Station.

RIGHT:

The multipurposed duties of the USAF, Iraq

Technical Sergeant Anthony Williams, of the 506th Expeditionary Civil Engineer Squadron at Kirkuk Regional Air Base, Iraq, welds together a school desk for local children, illustrating the broad duties of USAF Airmen.

FAR TOP RIGHT:

Target ball repair, Iraq

Aircraft mechanics replace a multispectural targeting system ball on an MQ-1B Predator drone at Ali Base, Iraq. The MQ-1B provides close-air combat support for intelligence, surveillance, and reconnaissance missions.

FAR BOTTOM RIGHT:

57th Maintenance Group competitions

The 57th Maintenance Group holds competitions to give Airmen an opportunity to showcase their technical expertise to their peers and base leaders. Here Senior Airman Christina Phillips secures munitions on an F-16 Fighting Falcon during the Load Crew of the Quarter Competition at Nellis Air Force Base, Nevada.

TOP LEFT:

Covid-19 support, Germany
Senior Airman Juan Castro, 86th Logistics Readiness Squadron fuels distribution operator, pulls up a hydrant outlet coupling after refueling an aircraft at Ramstein Air Base, Germany. Castro's fuel support has enabled the transport of hundreds of testing swabs during the Covid-19 pandemic.

LEFT:

Heavy weapons operations, Operation Iraqi Freedom
Senior Airman Elizabeth Gonzalez cleans a .50-caliber machine gun at the armory at Sather Air Base, Iraq. Airman Gonzales is a heavy weapons operator with the 447th Expeditionary Security Forces Squadron and is one of a few security forces members there qualified on the .50 cal.

ABOVE:

Chemical threat training exercise, Qatar
Senior Airman Taylor Lahteine, assigned to the 379th Expeditionary Civil Engineer Squadron, operates a Remotec Andros F6A Remote Ordnance Neutralization System during a joint chemical threat training exercise at Al Udeid Air Base, Qatar. The robot, which has chemical detection capability, is used to perform the initial reconnaissance on an unknown object in the exercise.

Bagram Airfield runway, Afghanistan
Airmen from the 577th Expeditionary Prime Base Engineer Emergency Force Squadron stationed at Al Udeid Air Base, Qatar, remove rubber from the runway at Bagram Airfield, Afghanistan. Foam and biodegradable solvents are used to strip the rubber left by taking off and landing aircraft at Bagram in support of Operation Freedom's Sentinel and NATO's Resolute Support missions.

LEFT:

RADR exercise, Kuwait

Senior Airman Zaldy Edjan of the 386th Expeditionary Civil Engineer Squadron, a water fuel systems maintenance technician, shovels dirt from a wheel saw during rapid airfield damage recovery (RADR) training at Ali Al Salem Air Base, Kuwait. RADR training teaches Airmen how to rebuild a damaged runway in a short amount of time to get planes back in the air.

ABOVE:

Ordnance and munitions training

An Explosive Ordnance Disposal Airman assigned to the 812th Civil Engineer Squadron, 412th Test Wing (TW), prepares unexploded ordnance and training munitions for demolition at the Precision Impact Range Area (PIRA) at Edwards Air Force Base, California. The 412th TW uses the PIRA to conduct weapons tests and payload drops during flight tests.

RIGHT:

K-9 and handler exercise, Iraq

Senior Airman William Bailey, a military working dog handler attached to the Army's 1st Cavalry Division, keeps Robby, an explosives detection dog, fit by exercising with him on an obstacle course at Camp Taji, Iraq. Such units help protect both civilians and military personnel by acting as an early warning system on the contents of suspect objects.

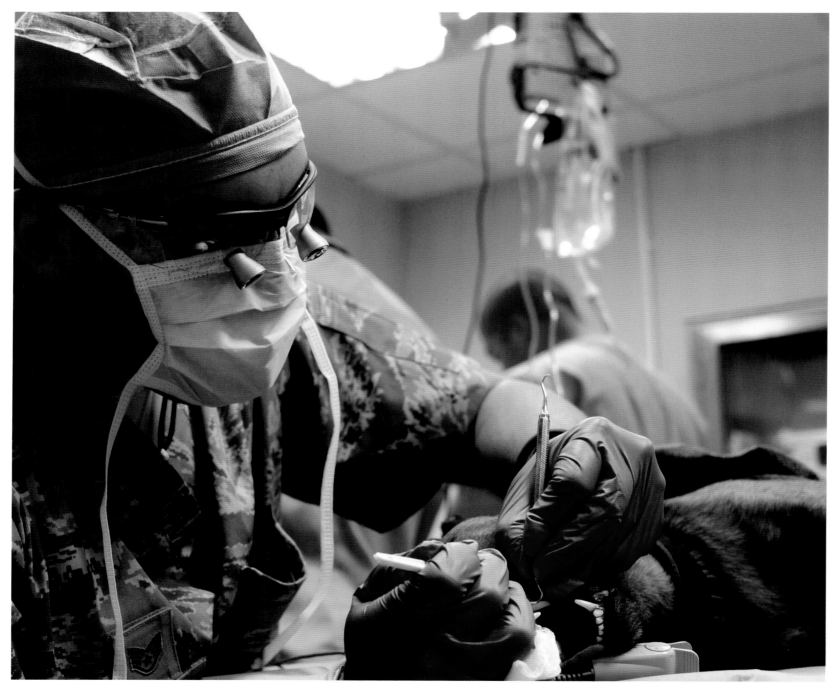

LEFT:

Military working dog gets its teeth cleaned
Staff Sergeant Gregory Johnson of the 386th Expeditionary Medical Support Squadron removes plaque from a military working dog's (MWD) teeth during a dental cleaning. MWD Frida is with the 386th Expeditionary Security Forces Squadron. MWDs receive routine medical care so they can aid their human military partners in the fight against the Islamic State terrorist group.

RIGHT:

Live fire training, Japan
Senior Airman Eric Poole, a 374th Civil Engineer Squadron (CES) firefighter, battles a simulated aircraft fire during live-fire training at Yokota Air Base, Japan. Aircraft live-fire training is conducted periodically throughout the year to ensure Airmen and civilians with the 374th CES and 374th Maintenance Squadron repair and reclamation section are always prepared to combat aircraft fuel fires.

ABOVE:

Exercise Point Blank, England

US Air Force Pararescuemen of the 57th Rescue Squadron recover a pilot during exercise Point Blank at the Stanford Training Area, England. Exercise Pointblank is a regularly occurring joint large-force exercise planned and co-hosted by the 48th Fighter Wing and the Royal Air Force.

RIGHT:

"Jolly Green" Airmen conduct rescue training, Japan

Technical Sergeant Jewel Steamer fires a .50-caliber machine-gun from an HH-60G Pave Hawk helicopter during a training exercise near Okinawa, Japan. The Air Force has used Pave Hawks in a wide array of search and rescue missions that range from combat operations in Iraq and Afghanistan to Hurricane Katrina relief and Operation Tomodachi in Japan, which provided relief after the 2011 Tohoku earthquake and tsunami.

Origins of the Air Force

The lineage of the United States Air Force can be traced back to 1 August 1907 and the establishment of the Aeronautical Division of the US Army's Signal Corps. Two years later, Orville and Wilbur Wright delivered "Aeroplane No. 1" to the Army for $30,000. On 8 December 1913, over six years later, the 1st Aero Squadron was formed. Despite the reluctance of many Army leaders to embrace the airplane as a viable instrument of war and the squadron's poor showing in the Army's efforts to capture Pancho Villa in 1916–17, important technological advancements had been made in the first decade of American military aviation.

This trajectory would continue through the first half of the twentieth century. World War I (1914–18) would play no small part, both from the standpoint of technology and tactics. By war's end, the airplane had proven its worth as an effective vehicle for reconnaissance and intelligence gathering, but its capabilities as a weapon of war remained to be seen. Nevertheless, such aviators as Brigadier General Billy Mitchell embraced the concept of strategic bombing and would be among the "Army Air Corps'" chief architects during the interwar period.

After winning equality with the infantry and artillery in July 1926, the Engineering Division (later renamed the Materiel Division) would work closely with American industry and the NASA antecedent, the National Advisory Committee for Aeronautics, throughout the interwar period to make substantial advances in aircraft engines, airframes, wing designs, flight controls, and landing gear. The outbreak of World War II in Europe mobilized and expanded the American aviation industry and gave the Army cause to significantly expand the Air Corps.

LEFT:
The first members of the early Air Force
Master Sergeant Carl T. Hale, one of the first enlisted men in the Aviation Section of the Army Signal Corps, was assigned to the Wright section, first at College Park, Maryland, and later at Texas City, Texas. This photo, one of a series, depicts early flying activities at Texas City. Hale retired in 1938 after more than 30 years of service in Army aviation.

LEFT:

First pilots
The first pilots, Lieutenants Frank P. Lahm (right) and Benjamin D. Foulois of the Aeronautical Division, US Signal Corps. Lahm would rise to the rank of Brigadier General and served as Chief of Staff during World War I to Foulois, who rose to the rank of Major General and commanded the Air Service.

RIGHT:

The National Aeroplane Fund
The National Aeroplane Fund was sanctioned by the Aero Club of America in response to perceived military and political disinterest in aeronautics. Established in the summer of 1915, the group lobbied Congress to increase funding for military aeronautics and independently instituted programs to develop aviation in the National Guard and formed a civilian aviation reserve.

LEFT:

The first bomber plane

Phil Parmalee and Lieutenant Myron Crissy (left) with the first live bomb, in a Wright plane, Los Angeles. Crissy, assisted by Marine Lieutenant J.W. McCaskey and the research of Lieutenant Paul Beck, designed and dropped the first aircraft munition at the International Air Meet in January 1911 in San Francisco, California.

ABOVE:

The Wright Military Flyer

The Wright Military Flyer was a development of the Flyer III aircraft of 1905. Known as the "Model A" in later years, it had a 35hp (26kW) engine and seating for two. It first arrived in crates at Fort Myer, Virginia on 20 August 1908 and was assembled there, from where it was transported on the back of a wagon to the launch site. Here Lieutenant Thomas E. Selfridge (left) and Orville Wright (right) wait to take off on the fateful flight of 17 September 1908 at Fort Myer.

The dangers of early flight
One of the Wrights in an August 1908 pre-trial flight at Fort Myer, Virginia. Sadly, the 1908 flyer's trial culminated in the first powered aircraft fatality when Lieutenant Thomas E. Selfridge died of injuries sustained in a crash on 17 September 1908; Orville Wright suffered several broken bones and injured his back.

Wright Military Flyer and launching derrick
On 27 July 1909, nearly a year after the crash at Fort Myer, Virginia, the Wrights returned with a new Model A flyer for the Army to test. With President William Howard Taft and some 15,000 spectators in attendance, Lieutenant Frank Lahm accompanied Wilbur Wright on the flight.

LEFT:

Early reconnaissance
An airplane Graflex camera in action, *c.* 1917–18. The aerial reconnaissance conducted during World War I marked the first time that technologically gathered intelligence was more prized than human intelligence.

RIGHT:

Join the Air Service!
The early design for the Air Force emblem on a World War I propaganda poster from 1917. Although the term "Air Service" had been in use in France since June 1917 to describe aviation units attached to the American Expeditionary Force, the United States Army Air Service was only established as an independent but temporary wartime branch of the War Department by two executive orders of President Woodrow Wilson the following year.

FAR TOP RIGHT:

Engineering fuselage repair shop, France
American Expeditionary Force (AEF) Air Service members working in the engineering fuselage repair shop at the 2nd Air Instructional Center, Tours Aerodrome, in 1918.

FAR BOTTOM RIGHT:

Fueling a Nieuport, France
Members of the AEF Air Service fueling a French Nieuport fighter at the 3rd Air Instructional Center, Issoudun Aerodrome, in 1918.

LEFT:
1st Aero Squadron, France
The members of the 1st Aero Squadron at Julvecourt Aerodrome, France in November 1918. The squadron was formed as a response to Mexico's revolutionary violence in early 1913 and consisted of nine airplanes, nine officers, and 51 enlisted men organized into two companies. They saw activity in Mexico in 1916–17 before joining the fight in France in World War I.

RIGHT:
96th Aero Squadron
Two flyers of the 96th Aero Squadron posing in front of one of the squadron's Breguet 14 B.2 bombers in 1918. Note the Vickers machine gun mounted on the side of the fuselage. The gun was synchronized to fire only when the bullet would miss the propeller blade in front of it, an indication of the advancing nature of military technology at the time.

FAR LEFT:

The American Eagles
A US Army Air Service
propaganda poster from
World War I (*c.* 1918) invites
registration to the then young
branch of the Army. The
poster depicts the American
bald eagle locked in combat
with a black eagle, which
represented the one on
Imperial Germany's coat
of arms.

LEFT:

**Captain Edward
Vernon Rickenbacker**
Captain Edward Vernon
"Eddie" Rickenbacker posing
with his Nieuport 28 C1.
The fuselage bears the 94th
Aero Squadron's "Hat in the
Ring" insignia.

RIGHT:

**Major General
William L. Kenly**
Major General William L.
Kenly, Director of Military
Aeronautics, stands in the
gondola of a hot air balloon
in 1918. Shortly before his
retirement in 1919, Kenly
was placed in command of
the US Army Air Service.

LEFT:

Martin MB-1 bomber
An interested crowd gather
to see the Martin MB-1
bomber on its arrival with
the Air Service in October
1918. An order for six had
been increased to 50 that
month, but after the Armistice
this was cut back to the 10
delivered, although this was
too late for them to serve in
World War I.

ABOVE:

Sopwith Camels, France
The 148th Aero Squadron,
AEF Air Service in Petite
Sythe, France, prepare their
Sopwith Camels for a raid
on the German trenches on
6 August 1918 during the
closing stages of World War I.

RIGHT:

Ruth Law
Famed female aviator Ruth
Law was the first woman
allowed to wear a military
uniform. Despite being
denied approval to fly combat
missions, she raised money to
support the war through flying
demonstrations.

8th Photo Section, France
The AEF Air Service, 8th Photo Section, during World War I. Photographic sections were assigned to observation squadrons and were responsible for printing the aerial images captured by the squadrons as well as assembling composite maps for analysis.

1st Air Depot Camera Shop, France
Members of the AEF Air Service, 1st Air Depot Camera Shop, hard at work at Colombey-les-Belles Aerodrome in France in January 1919. The 1st Air Depot was an important installation that equipped arriving Air Service units; the Camera Shop maintained and repaired Air Service reconnaissance cameras.

FAR LEFT:

Training in the Engineering Engine Repair Shop, France
Air Service members receiving training in the Engineering Engine Repair Shop (2nd Air Instructional Center, Tours Aerodrome, France) stop to pose for a photo in 1918. On completing their training here, Air Service Airmen were deployed to their combat field assignments.

LEFT:

Salmson 2A.2, France
This Salmson 2A.2, a French-manufactured reconnaissance biplane, of the 1st Aero Squadron of the AEF Air Service flies over France in 1918. The Salmson 2A.2 was one of the first aircraft to be flown into action by the Air Service during World War I.

LEFT:

Brigadier General William L. "Billy" Mitchell
Widely regarded as the father of the USAF, the combative Mitchell was the chief advocate of tactical and strategic bombing in the Air Service. He would adamantly press the Army and Congress for increased investment in airpower development until his death in 1936.

RIGHT:

Keystone B-6A
A Keystone B-6A bomber assigned to the 1st Bomb Squadron, 9th Bomb Group. The B-6A was the last biplane bomber acquired by the Army Air Corps (another precursor name for the USAF, used between 1926 and 1941). A total of 39 were produced and delivered between August 1931 and January 1932.

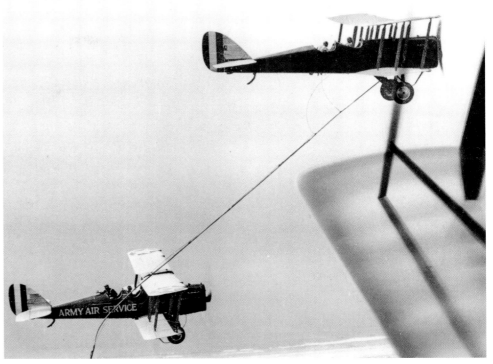

FAR LEFT:

Curtiss B-2 Condors

A formation of Curtiss B-2 Condor bombers from the 11th Bomb Squadron, 7 Bomb Group, high above the beaches of Atlantic City, New Jersey, *c*. 1929. The rapid advancement of flight technology in this period, however, rendered the B-2 obsolete by 1934.

LEFT:

In the cockpit of the only Curtiss XA-8

The front cockpit instrument board of the Curtiss XA-8 prototype, the only plane with this designation, on 15 June 1931. Thirteen more service test XA-8s were ordered, 11 of which were redesignated as A-8s. The A-8 was an all-metal monoplane attack aircraft procured to replace the much slower, outmoded Curtiss A-3 Falcon biplane.

ABOVE:

The first aerial refueling

On 27 June 1923, a de Havilland DH-4B tanker dangled a hose down to another DH-4B to grab over Rockwell Field, San Diego, California. In the tanker, 1st Lieutenant Frank W. Seifert holds the hose in the rear cockpit while the pilot, 1st Lieutenant Virgile Hine, is in the front. Captain Lowell H. Smith flew the receiver and 1st Lieutenant John P. Richter handled the hose.

Douglas C-1

Douglas C-1, No. 79 (serial number (s/n) 25-433), in flight in April 1926. The C-1 could transport six to eight passengers (note the passenger windows in the photo) or up to 2500lb (1134kg) of cargo; it was the Army Air Corps' first cargo plane, though it ended up serving a variety of purposes amid Air Corps experimentation.

LEFT:

Martin MB-2 bomber
A Martin MB-2 bomber being trailed by a pursuit plane, which veers off to rehearse its attack. The Glenn L. Martin Company produced 130 MB-2s between 1920 and 1922. The bomber was an updated version of the NBS-1 the Air Service used in World War I.

RIGHT:

Navigation precision
An Atlantic-Fokker C-2 Bird of Paradise after its repainting in 1928. This was one of three procured by the Army Air Corps for testing new navigation technologies. Just weeks after Charles Lindbergh's famed transatlantic flight from New York City to Paris in 1927, 1st Lieutenants Lester Maitland and Albert Hegenberger completed the first flight over the Pacific, flying from Oakland, California to Wheeler Field, Hawaii.

RIGHT:

Douglas C-33 cockpit
The cockpit instrument board of the first Douglas C-33 (s/n 33-70), March 1937. The C-33 was the predecessor to the C-47s built during World War II. The C-33 could transport up to 2400lb (1098kg) of cargo or 12 soldiers along with their packs.

FAR RIGHT:

Douglas C-33
A Douglas C-33 (s/n 36-70) stands at Wright Field, Ohio (known today as Wright-Patterson Air Force Base), September 1936. Only 18 C-33s were produced before the C-39, a more powerful and stable version of the C-33, started to be built. A Martin B-10B bomber stands in the background.

The Air Force
in World War II

After the Japanese Naval Air Service attacked US Naval Station Pearl Harbor, Hawaii on 7 December 1941, the US entered into World War II. Understanding the inevitability of America's entry into the war, President Franklin D. Roosevelt had been expanding America's armed forces since the French defeat by the Germans in June 1940. A year later, Army Regulation 95-5 created the Army Air Forces (USAAF), which encompassed all of the Army's aviation commands and placed them under Major General Henry "Hap" Arnold.

General Arnold focused his energy on the ramping-up of American industrial production, the Army Air Forces' flight training infrastructure, and its aircraft research and development efforts. As a result, over the course of the war, American factories would work around the clock to produce 324,750 aircraft; the Flying Training Command would train almost 200,000 pilots as well as hundreds of thousands of navigators, bombardiers, gunners, and other aircrew specialists; and researchers across the country designed and tested myriad technological advancements, such as radars, radios, rockets, jet engines, aviation fuel, and specialized munitions.

The USAAF operated in Europe—including in France, Italy, and Germany—in North Africa, and across Asia, including in Japan, Burma (now Myanmar), and China. Their Airmen flew a total 2,352,800 bomber and fighter missions against determined enemies. In those missions, they dropped 1.6 million tons (1.45 million tonnes) of munitions in the European theater of operations and 502,781 tons (456,115 tonnes) in the Pacific. During World War II, some 2,253,000 Americans served in the USAAF. Of those, 88,119 would not return home.

LEFT:
P-47s on their way to the Pacific theater
A deckload of USAAF Republic P-47N Thunderbolt fighters on the flight deck of the escort carrier USS *Casablanca* (CVE-55) in July 1945. The planes were loaded at Naval Air Station Alameda, California and were bound for Guam. After the recapture of Guam in August 1944, the island would become an important jumping-off point for USAAF missions against Japanese targets.

**"Honey Chile" crew,
England**
American pilot Robert W.
Biesecker and his crew stand
by their B-17 Flying Fortress
bomber "Honey Chile" at
a US 8th Air Force station
in England in 1943. With
them are their two mascots,
a dog named Scrappy and a
monkey called Joe. Scrappy
was presented to the crew
while training in the US and
accompanied them on their
transatlantic flight to England.

WASP pilots at Love Field
Women Airforce Service Pilots
(WASPs) were USAAF-trained
pilots who ferried 12,652
aircraft from factories to 122
air bases, coached other pilots,
and supported anti-aircraft
defense training during World
War II. Their activities aimed
to free up male pilots for
combat. WASP was actually
a civilian women pilots'
organization whose members
were United States federal
civil service employees and,
as such, these women had no
military standing.

Airacobras in formation
The Bell P-39 Airacobra
was one of the first pursuit
planes of the USAAF at the
outset of World War II. The
P-39 was unique in that its
engine was located behind the
cockpit. The Airacobra saw
combat throughout the world,
particularly in the southwest
Pacific, Mediterranean, and
Russian theaters in close air-
support missions.

Texans in the Arizona sky
Two USAAF North American
AT-6C-NT Texan trainers in
flight near Luke Field, Arizona
in 1943. During World War
II, USAAF and Navy pilots
performed their advanced
training in this versatile, two-
seat, single-engine aircraft.

LEFT:

Armed to the teeth
The P-47 Thunderbolt
was a rugged and versatile
fighter-bomber aircraft
capable of taking an unusual
amount of abuse. It was a
capable escort fighter that
proved an effective close
air-support platform, able
to strafe and bomb targets
when the opportunity arose.

ABOVE:

Stinson L-5G Sentinel
The Stinson L-5G Sentinel
was the second most widely
used USAAF liaison aircraft
of World War II. Sentinels
were used for reconnaissance,
aeromedical evacuations,
delivering supplies, laying
communications wire,
spotting enemy targets, and
transporting personnel.

RIGHT:

**Lockheed P-38 Lightnings
in formation**
A group of USAAF Lockheed
P-38 Lightning fighters in flight
as they train for combat duty,
Burbank, California in 1943.
Similar to the P-47, the P-38,
or "the Forked-Tail Devil,"
as nicknamed by German
pilots, proved a valuable
multipurpose fighter-bomber.

**Bombing a German
aircraft factory**
On 9 October 1943, the B-17
Flying Fortresses of the 303rd
Bomb Group, US 8th Air
Force, obliterated the Focke-
Wulf aircraft manufacturing
plant at Marienburg,
Germany. Clear weather and
unlimited visibility helped
enable this raid's exceptional
accuracy, aimed at disrupting
production of such aircraft as
Fw-190s.

**The Memphis Belle
and crew, England**
The crew of the "Memphis
Belle" B-17F bomber after
completing their 25th mission
on 7 June 1943. A combat
tour for a USAAF bomber
crew entailed completing
25 missions, no small feat
considering that only a
quarter of 8th Air Force
bomber crew members
finished such a tour. The
Memphis Belle was one of
the first USAAF B-17 heavy
bombers to do so, having
successfully undertaken
missions in France, Germany,
and the Netherlands.

B-17s depart on a mission
B-17 Flying Fortresses leave
vapor trails while heading
towards occupied Europe on
a bombing mission. Primarily
used for daylight attacks
against enemy infrastructure
and industry, more than
640,000 tons (650,000 tonnes)
of bombs were dropped by
B-17s during World War II.

**Reloading for the
next mission**
A P-51 Mustang ground
crew loading the fighter's six
.50-caliber machine guns.
The P-51 is among the best-
known fighters of World War
II. With excellent range and
maneuverability, the P-51
served primarily as a long-
range escort fighter as well
as a ground attack fighter-
bomber. Mustangs served
in nearly every combat zone
during World War II.

ABOVE:

Landing in Salerno, Italy

The 817th Engineer Aviation Battalion unloading vehicles from the USS *LST-391* during landing operations in Salerno, Italy in 1943. In the foreground is a USAAF-operated Supermarine Spitfire Mk.VB nose-down in the surf, reportedly having been shot down by mistake by American anti-aircraft guns.

RIGHT:

The 2nd Bomb Group at work

A P-38J Lightning escort with a damaged engine out in front of the B-17s of 2nd Bomb Group, 5th Bomb Wing, 15th Air Force. The 2nd Bomb Group participated in strategic bombing operations in support of the invasion of Italy in September 1943.

FAR LEFT:

Traveling in style

US and Chinese troops head to China on an Air Transport Command (ATC) aircraft with supplies for the Chinese 6th Army. The 10th Air Force established the India-China Wing (ICW) of the ATC to supply China from India, above the Himalayan Mountains.

LEFT TOP:

Bombing a Japanese warehouse

A B-25 Mitchell medium bomber of the 1st Air Commando Group (ACG) bombs Japanese military warehouses in 1944. The 1st ACG gave close air support, bomber, and air transport services for British and Indian units fighting behind Japanese lines in Burma.

LEFT BOTTOM:

"Flying Tigers" at work

Crewmen of Claire Chennault's "Flying Tigers" work on the Browning machine guns of the P-40 Warhawks (background). The tactical successes the American Volunteer Group (AVG) were a bright spot in the dismal opening months of the war.

RIGHT:

Striking at Japanese targets

A 14th Air Force (AF) B-24 Liberator bombs a target in French Indochina. The 14th AF is credited with destroying 2315 Japanese aircraft, 356 bridges, 1225 locomotives, and 712 railroad cars.

69

Operation Tidal Wave, Romania

B-24 Liberators of the US 15th USAAF bombing the Concordia Vega oil refinery, Ploesti, Romania, in May 1944. The costly mission was a part of Operation Tidal Wave, aimed at denying Germany and its allies fuel from the Romanian refineries.

RIGHT:

The ground crew inspect their B-24

A B-24 Liberator of the 98th Bomb Group, who were involved in Operation Tidal Wave. The 98th Bomb Group was one of five to take part in low-level massed raids on nine different Romanian oil refineries. The oil lost in the raids was significant, but was quickly replaced.

LEFT:

Cockpit of the C-46A

The C-46A Commando was a mainstay in airlifting supplies over the heights of the Himalayan Mountains, known as "the Hump" to Allied flyers. In Europe, the C-46 was used to drop American paratroopers in Operation Varsity on 24 March 1945. This photo was taken in 1944.

RIGHT:

Airmen reloading the P-47's machine guns

By the latter months of 1944, US troops had pushed well into France and were closing in on the Japanese main islands. The P-47 Thunderbolt was active in both theaters, providing close air support for ground troops and escorting US bombers.

LEFT:

Tuskegee Airmen of the 100th Fighter Squadron
Airmen pose in front of Captain Andrew "Jug" Turner's (second from the right) P-51 Mustang, "Skipper's Darlin' III," in August 1944. The Tuskegee Airmen were the first black military aviators in the US Army Air Corps.

ABOVE:

Airmen rolling a bomb
A pair of USAAF ground crewmen move a large bomb at an ammunition dump. The ground crew filled a variety of jobs, all of which contributed to the organization and operation of the airfield to which they were assigned.

RIGHT:

Tuskegee Airmen prepped for their mission, Italy
Pilots exit the parachute room in Ramitelli, Italy in 1945. The 332nd Fighter Group of black servicemen, 15th Air Force, would receive a Distinguished Unit Citation for their mission escorting a B-17 bombing mission on the Daimler-Benz tank factory in Berlin.

ABOVE:
A downed C-47 Skytrain, Belgium
A C-47 crashed in Belgium after dropping supplies to besieged American troops at Bastogne in December 1944. The supplies delivered by USAAF C-47s helped the troops of the 28th Infantry Division, 82nd Airborne, and 101st Airborne Divisions keep the Germans at bay until the US 3rd Army arrived.

RIGHT:
The multipurposed Douglas C-47 Skytrain
The C-47 was an all-purpose cargo aircraft that the USAAF used to transport supplies, tow gliders, and drop paratroopers. They are probably best known for these latter two tasks thanks to Operations Overlord and Market Garden.

FAR LEFT:

A-20s wreaking Havoc, France
Douglas A-20 Havoc light bombers strike the Pointe du Hoc strongpoint in Normandy in May 1944. Though designed as an attack bomber for operations against ground troops and installations, its speed and maneuverability made it a versatile aircraft.

LEFT:

Northrop P-61B Black Widow
A Northrop P-61B Black Widow of the 420th Night Fighter Squadron in its shiny black paint is out of place in the daytime skies. The first P-61s arrived in the European and Pacific theaters in March 1944, intercepting enemy bombers and bombing and strafing trains and enemy vehicles.

Operation Dragoon, France
Troops of the 1st Airborne
Task Force, 7th Army, leaving
their gliders to meet up at
the checkpoint area after
landing in La Motte, France
in August 1944. Operation
Dragoon was a second set of
US-led amphibious landings,
after Operation Overlord, in
southern France.

FAR RIGHT:
**A C-47A during
Operation Varsity, France**
A C-47A of the 32nd Troop
Carrier Squadron returning
to Poix Airfield, France from
its Operation Varsity sortie in
March 1945. This operation
was the largest single-day
airborne undertaking in
history, landing some 21,000
troops in the German
Rhineland, behind the
retreating German army.

LEFT:

B-26 Marauder and its crew
The B-26 Marauder known as "Ginger" (pictured) departed on a bombing mission in April 1944 and did not return. It was damaged by anti-aircraft fire and the crew was forced to bail out of the aircraft near Berck-sur-Mer in France and were taken prisoner.

OPPOSITE TOP:

Waco CG-4, France
A glider of the 1st Allied Airborne Army sits on Poix airfield, France as C-46s, C-47s, and gliders fill the sky. Operation Varsity was intended to secure bridgeheads over the Rhine river in order to aid the advance of Allied ground troops.

OPPOSITE BOTTOM:

Airborne troops preparing to depart
US paratroopers prepare to board C-46 Commandos for the commencement of Operation Varsity, 24 March 1945. These paratroopers would be dropped near the city of Wesel.

FAR RIGHT:

B-26s in action over Europe
A squadron of B-26 Marauder medium bombers dropping their payload. USAAF B-26s began flying combat missions in the southwest Pacific in the spring of 1942, though the majority would subsequently be assigned to the European and Mediterranean theaters.

A B-26 in flames after flak hit, Germany

USAAF B-26 "Gratis Gladys" (tail number (t/n) 43-34565) of the 497th Bomb Squadron, 344th Bomb Group, 9th Air Force in flames after taking anti-aircraft flak to its left engine during a raid on Erkelenz, Germany on 26 February 1945. All eight crew members died in the crash.

An earlier B-25 in flight

A North American Aviation, Inc. B-25C Mitchell bomber in flight. The B-25Cs were produced in Inglewood, California. The B-25, made famous by the Doolittle Raid in April 1942, was originally intended for medium altitude bombing and was widely employed in the Pacific, attacking Japanese airfields and beach emplacements at treetop levels, strafing, and skip-bombing enemy shipping.

ABOVE:

The bombing of Kobe, Japan
Incendiary bombs from
USAAF B-29 Superfortresses
fall on the seaport of Kobe in
June 1945. The concentration
of Japanese military factories
in densely populated centers
made the attacks damaging to
both industry and the morale
of the Japanese people.

RIGHT:

A P-400 at Guadalcanal
A USAAF P-400 Airacobra of
the 80th Fighter Squadron,
8th Fighter Group parked
at Henderson Field,
Guadalcanal in the Solomon
Islands. The original,
Japanese-constructed airstrip
was taken over by US troops
and named Henderson Field.

LEFT:

Paratroopers of the Pacific

Paratroopers of the 511th Parachute Infantry exiting a C-46 Commando. The 11th Airborne saw its first action in the battles of Leyte and Luzon in the Philippines, where they conducted a daring raid on a Japanese internment camp, helped liberate more than 2000 Allied internees in Los Baños, and aided in the retaking of Manila (both also in the Philippines). The 11th Airborne was also a part of the US force that occupied post-war Japan.

RIGHT:

Wounded soldiers return stateside, Japan

A Douglas R5D-3 Skymaster in Okinawa, Japan prepares for takeoff on 6 May 1945. The plane is loaded with wounded soldiers being evacuated back to the US.

LEFT:

Preparing a "Special Delivery," Saipan, Northern Mariana Islands

The aircrew of the B-29 Superfortress "Special Delivery," 497th Bomb Group, at Isley Field, Saipan in 1944, prepares the bomber for its next mission on the Japanese main islands.

ABOVE:

The war in the Pacific draws to a close, Northern Mariana Islands

The crew of the B-29 Superfortress "Enola Gay" dropped the first atom bomb—"Little Boy"—on Hiroshima, Japan on 6 August 1945. Colonel Paul W. Tibbets Jr. (center), the pilot for the mission, stands with the crew in the Mariana Islands. On 9 August, a second atomic bomb was dropped on Nagasaki. Only six days later did Japan surrender, ending World War II.

From the Korean War to the Balkans

The matter of the Army Air Forces being its own, independent branch of the US Armed Forces was postponed until the conclusion of World War II. If there had been any doubt that it should be its own autonomous arm, its operations during the war made clear that it could and should be. Throughout 1946 and early 1947, Generals Henry "Hap" Arnold and Carl "Tooey" Spaatz worked to establish the infrastructures necessary for its independence, which it gained on 18 September 1947, becoming the "USAF."

It was the USAAF that dropped the atomic bombs on Hiroshima and Nagasaki in 1945. These events proved formative to US Cold War strategy, as illustrated by the USAF's acquisition of such nuclear bomb-delivering strategic bombers as the B-36 Peacemaker, B-47 Stratojet, B-52 Stratofortress, and the B-58 Hustler. Yet while deterrence may have prevented a US–USSR nuclear war, the USAF was ill-equipped for the limited, conventional wars over Korea (1950–53) and Vietnam (1961–75).

The growth of the USAF's Intercontinental Ballistic Missile inventory over the course of the 1960s, the de-escalation of the Cold War, and the Air Force's struggles in Vietnam compelled Air Force leaders to return their focus to standard warfighting. Armament and aircraft development was guided by new technologies used in Vietnam, such as precision-guided munitions, or by deficiencies in training or capabilities, such as more realistic combat training, dog-fighting aircraft including the F-15 Eagle and the F-16 Fighting Falcon, stealth capabilities to destroy air-defense systems, and an effective close air-support aircraft in the case of the A-10 Thunderbolt II. Air campaigns in the Gulf War (1990–91) and in the Balkans (1993–95, 1999) put the power of these advances on display.

LEFT:
Flying the world's fastest manned aircraft
Major Brian Shul in the cockpit of the SR-71 Blackbird. During the Vietnam War, Shul flew AT-28 Trojans on counter-insurgency missions. In 1973 he was shot down and severely burned in the crash. Against all odds, he returned to full flying status to pilot SR-71s.

The USAF is established

The National Security Act of 1947 established the legal groundwork for a separate, independent air force. Stuart Symington (far left) was sworn in as the first Secretary of the Air Force by Chief Justice Fred Vinson on 18 September 1947. General Carl "Tooey" Spaatz was sworn in as the first Chief of Staff of the Air Force on 26 September 1947.

RIGHT:

F-80, Korea

USAF F-80C fighter aircraft of the 16th Fighter Interceptor Squadron, 51st Fighter Interceptor Wing at Suwon Air Base, Korea in June 1951. The F-80 Shooting Star was the USAF jet fighter chosen for combat operations.

ABOVE:

The Berlin Airlift, Germany
Air Force C-47s and C-54s unloading their cargo at Templehof, Berlin, 1948. Soviet officials initiated the blockade of West Berlin on 24 June 1948 as a response to the Western-introduced Deutsche Mark as a new currency for West Germany, prompting the Allies to introduce Operation Vittles to supply and feed the citizens of West Berlin.

RIGHT:

Loading coal for West Berliners, Germany
A USAF C-54 being loaded with coal at RAF Fassberg during the Berlin Airlift operations. French, British, and American cargo planes brought between 5000 and 8000 tons (4540 and 7260 tonnes) of food and supplies per day to the city for well over a year, with the airlift ending on 30 September 1949.

German children watching a C-54 land, Germany

Excited children watch an Air Force C-54 preparing to land at Templehof Airport, West Berlin in 1948. At the height of Operation Vittles, cargo planes were reaching West Berlin every 30 seconds. USAF pilot Lieutenant Gail Halvorsen began dropping candy attached to makeshift parachutes from his plane, starting a trend adopted by other Allied pilots.

LEFT:

A Thunderjet on combat in Korea

A bomb-laden USAF Republic F-84E Thunderjet (t/n 49-2424) from the 310th Fighter-Bomber Squadron, 58th Fighter-Bomber Wing, taking off for a mission in Korea in December 1950. This aircraft would be shot down by anti-aircraft flak on 29 August 1952. After initial structural and engine teething problems during its debut in the late 1940s, the Thunderjet became the USAF's primary strike aircraft in Korea.

ABOVE:

F-86s in formation above Korea

A formation of F-86 Sabres from the 51st Fighter Interceptor Wing, US 5th Air Force, November 1952. The swept-wing Sabre provided a check on the advantages Russian MiG-15s demonstrated over UN aircraft in Korea throughout the early months of the war. The F-86 is considered one of the best and most important fighter aircraft in the Korean War, and is also rated highly in comparison with fighters of other eras.

An American fighter ace, Korea

Captain Joseph McConnell Jr. talks with his crew chief from his cockpit. McConnell would become the 27th ace of the Korean conflict. He was an F-86 Sabre pilot of the 51st Fighter Interceptor Wing, operating out of Suwon Air Base in South Korea. Flying aces are those pilots credited with shooting down five or more enemy aircraft in aerial combat.

Invaders releasing their payload, Korea

USAF Douglas B-26 Invader (only designated as B-26 between 1948 and 1965; otherwise it was known as the A-26) light bombers releasing their bombs over their target. The growing strength of North Korean air defenses, and the growing number of Russian MiG-15s in the skies, increasingly forced bombing raids to become night-time operations.

LEFT:

B-29s bombing a North Korean target
A flight of USAF B-29 Superfortresses release their loads on a daytime bombing raid in around 1951. In order to navigate the growing dangers over the North Korean skies, the time and altitude intervals between bomber streams were continuously altered to confuse enemy air-defense batteries.

RIGHT:

Flying Boxcars delivering their goods, Korea
USAF C-119s of the 314th Troop Carrier Group drops paratroops over Sunch'on, North Korea, during the UN attack on Pyongyang, 15–20 October 1950.

LEFT:

Rebranding the F-51, Korea
An "F-51D" (t/n 45-11742) of the 18th Fighter-Bomber Wing, 5th Air Force, taxiing through a pool of water at Chinhae Airfield, South Korea, September 1951. The F-51s used in Korea were P-51 Mustangs that the newly independent Air Force redesignated from "P," standing for "pursuit," to "F," standing for "fighter."

RIGHT:

Thunderchiefs refueling mid-air, Vietnam
Air Force F-105 Thunderchiefs over Vietnam, en route to their bomb target in January 1966. During their journey, they have to "pull up" to a flying "gas station," a KC-135 Stratotanker. "The Thud," as the F-105 was known by its pilots, was the only aircraft in Air Force history that had to be withdrawn from combat due to the fact that its loss rates were so high.

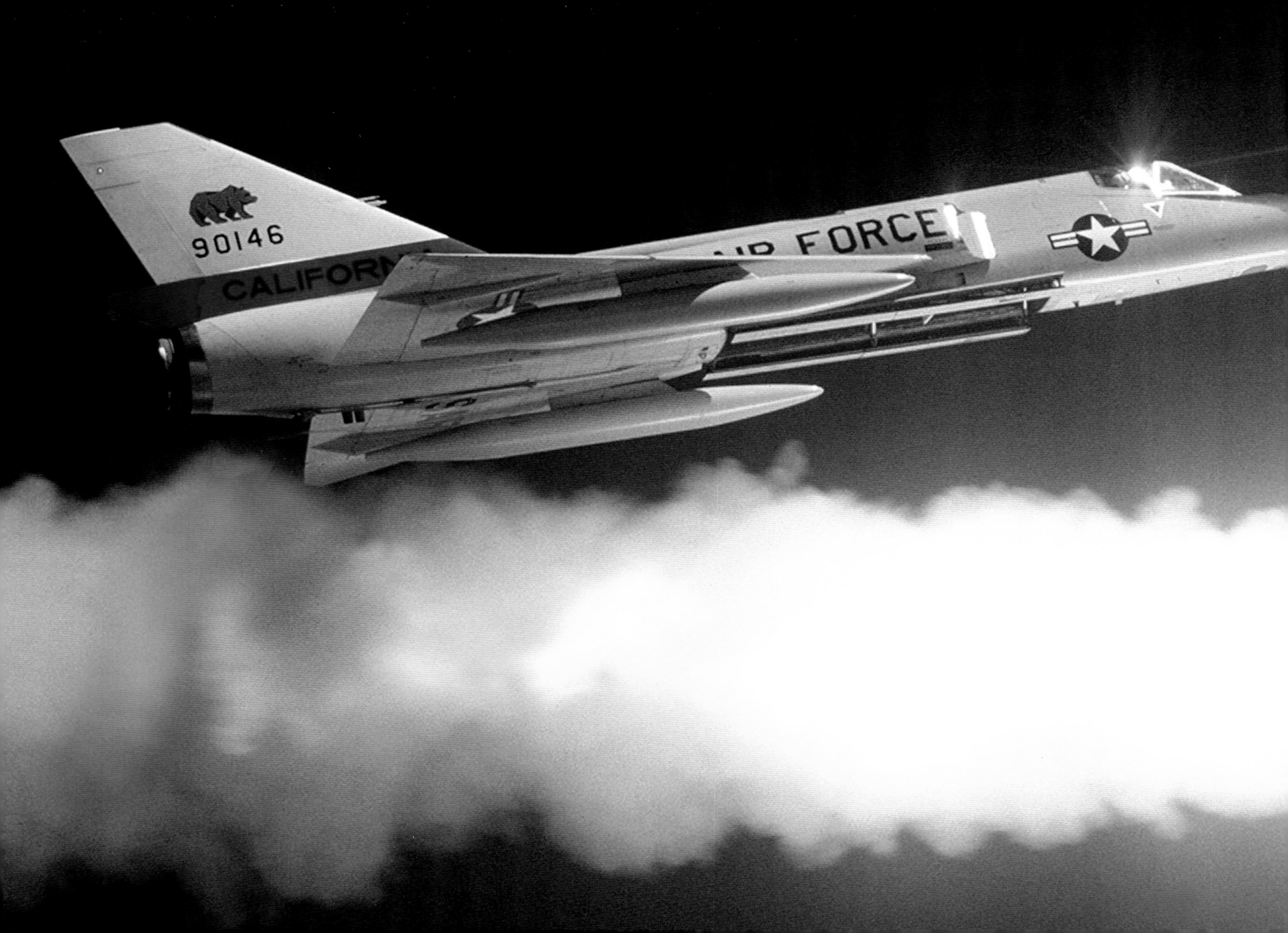
90146

F-106A Delta Dart
The all-weather interceptor F-106A Delta Dart of the 194th Fighter Interceptor Squadron, California Air National Guard, fires an ATR-2A missile during an exercise. In shot are the auxiliary fuel tanks on each wing and the internal bomb bay, still open after releasing its payload. The Delta Dart was the main all-weather interceptor aircraft of the USAF from the 1960s to the 1980s. Designed as the "Ultimate Interceptor," it proved to be the last dedicated one of its kind in USAF service to date.

LEFT:
McDonnell Douglas F-15 Eagle
The F-15 is a twin-engine, all-weather tactical fighter designed to gain air superiority over battlefield operations. The Eagle entered USAF service in January 1976. It is one of the most successful modern fighters, and has been exported to numerous other nations, including Japan, Israel, and Saudi Arabia.

RIGHT:
RB-57A Canberra
A Martin RB-57A Canberra (t/n 52-1447) of the 363rd Tactical Reconnaissance Group with the group's traditional checkerboard paint scheme on the tail. The Canberra entered service in 1953 during the Korean War as a medium bomber; it was the first jet engine bomber to be used in combat operations.

LEFT:

A Super Sabre in the heat of combat, Vietnam
An Air Force F-100D Super Sabre deploys a hail of rockets on a target in Vietnam in May 1967. The F-100D fighter-bomber was widely used in Vietnam for strike missions but was not especially effective for air-to-air combat scenarios.

ABOVE:

Special operations, Vietnam
An HH-53 helicopter of the 40th Aerospace Rescue and Recovery Squadron, seen from inside an HH-3E "Jolly Green Giant" of the 21st Special Operations Squadron, 1972. The HH-53 was an improved variant of the Marines' CH-3 transport helicopter, with both armor plating and armament to protect it from hostile forces during rescues of aircrews in a combat area.

LEFT:

O-1F Bird Dog, Vietnam
A USAF O-1F Bird Dog lands at an airfield in Vietnam, sometime around 1968. The O-1 was a USAF forward air-control aircraft, often flown by an experienced fighter pilot who could readily identify enemy activity. Pilots who successfully located enemy ground targets marked them with smoke rockets for attack by fighter-bombers.

RIGHT:

A-1E Skyraider, Vietnam
An A-1E Skyraider of the USAF 1st Air Commando Squadron attacking a ground target in Vietnam. This Skyraider was shot down in April 1966. The A-1 carried an assortment of weapons and could loiter over the battlefield for extended periods, providing close air support to ground forces, attacking enemy supply lines, and protecting rescue helicopters.

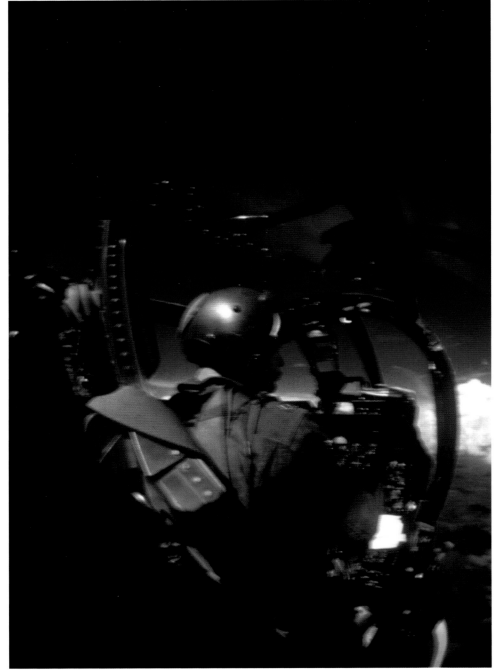

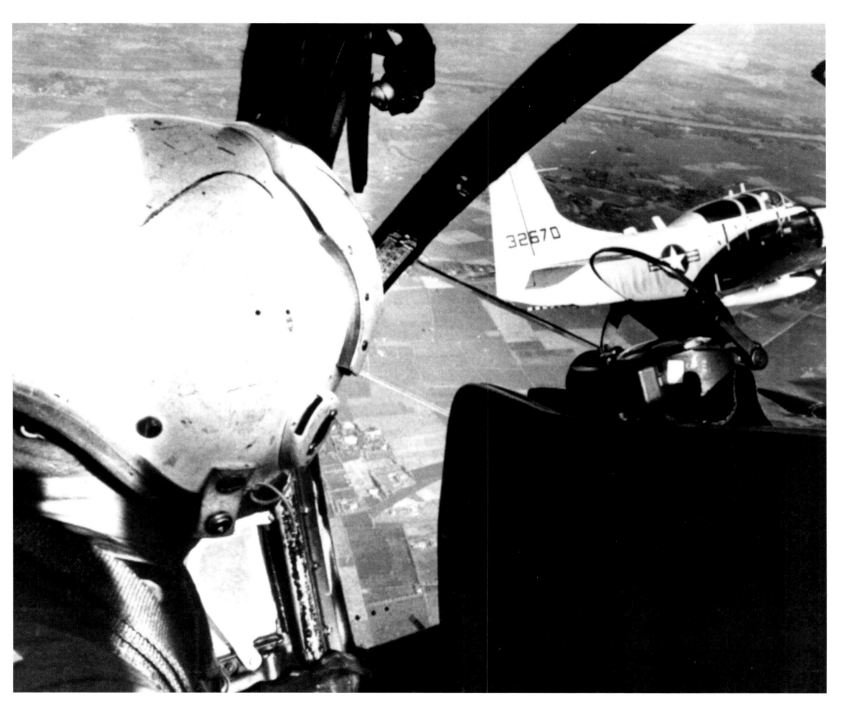

FAR LEFT:

Bombing targets over North Vietnam

Flying with a radar-jamming B-66 Destroyer, Air Force F-105 Thunderchief pilots bomb a military target through low clouds over the southern panhandle of North Vietnam in June 1966.

LEFT:

OV-10 Bronco, Vietnam

A USAF OV-10 Bronco pilot from the 23rd Tactical Air Support Squadron on a mission over Vietnam, 1972. The Bronco was developed in the 1960s as a special aircraft for counter-insurgency combat, and the USAF acquired it primarily to use as a forward air control (FAC) aircraft.

RIGHT:

1st Air Commando Squadron, Vietnam

A pair of A-1E Skyraiders of the 1st Air Commando Squadron on a sortie. The A-1E to the pilot's left (t/n 52-132670) crashed in July 1965. The Skyraider was an aircraft well suited for combating the guerrilla-style war waged by communist forces in Vietnam due to the large number of munitions it could carry and its ability to linger over the battle arena for long periods of time. This made it a powerful and effective weapon.

LEFT:

Air drops, Vietnam
An Air Force C-130 resupplies Thien Ngon Special Forces Civilian Irregular Defense Group Camp. In 1965, the C-130 Hercules, with its four turbo-prop engines, 15-ton (13.6 tonnes) payload, and its ability to quickly unload palletized cargo, dominated airlift operations in Vietnam.

ABOVE:

A C-130 delivers a different type of cargo, Vietnam
Viet Cong prisoners of war are delivered to Loc Ninh, Vietnam via the C-130 in the background (50th Tactical Airlift Squadron) in February 1973. The prisoners were exchanged for US and South Vietnamese POWs.

General Dynamics F-111 Aardvark, Vietnam
The F-111 Aardvark was a long-range, all-weather strike aircraft capable of navigating at low altitudes to destroy targets deep in enemy territory. The versatile F-111 entered the USAF inventory in 1967 and was retired in 1996.

Martin B-57 Canberra
A Canberra drops bombs somewhere over mountainous terrain in Vietnam. Armed with 2,800lb (1,300kg) of bombs on four external hardpoints, the Canberra was used extensively during the Vietnam War as a bomber.

Republic F-105 Thunderchief
A Thunderchief launches a stream of 2.75in (70mm) rockets at targets somewhere in rural Vietnam. Capable of reaching speeds of Mach 2, the Thunderchief conducted the majority of strike bombing missions during the early years of the Vietnam War.

F-100 Super Sabre, Vietnam
Airmen from the 435th Munitions Maintenance Squadron remove the chocks from an F-100 Super Sabre about to take off from Phan Rang Air Base, Vietnam. The F-100, beset by an array of issues, was phased out of combat operations by the F-105 and the F-4 Phantom II.

ABOVE:

Refueling the SR-71

A Boeing KC-135Q Stratotanker refueling a Lockheed SR-71 Blackbird from the 9th Strategic Reconnaissance Wing. The SR-71 is a long-range, high-altitude, Mach 3+ strategic reconnaissance aircraft that was operated by the USAF and NASA. KC-135 in-flight refueling specialists are highly trained and must have a steady hand and be cool under pressure.

RIGHT:

SR-71B Blackbird

The NASA SR-71B was the trainer version of the SR-71. This can be seen in the dual cockpit, which allows the instructor to fly the airplane. The SR-71 was developed as a black project (a highly classified military or defense project) from the Lockheed A-12 reconnaissance aircraft during the 1960s and its shape was based on that of the A-12, which was one of the first planes to be designed with a reduced radar cross-section.

C-130 Hercules, Panama
A USAF C-130 Hercules transport aircraft takes off from a landing strip in Panama during Operation Just Cause. The Hercules primarily performs the tactical portion of the USAF airlift missions and can operate from dirt airstrips to airdrop troops and equipment into hostile areas.

Operation Just Cause, Panama
A UH-60 Black Hawk helicopter being unloaded from a C-5 Galaxy transport aircraft during Operation Just Cause in Panama in 1989. Operation Just Cause was the invasion of Panama to oust the dictator Manuel Noriega—a long-time CIA intelligence asset—in December of that year.

LEFT:

Flying supplies into a besieged Sarajevo, Boznia and Herzegovina

An Air Force pilot, somewhere over Mannheim, Germany, flies a C-141 Starlifter loaded with supplies to Sarajevo, Bosnia and Herzegovina in 1993 during the Bosnian War. In this situation, his approach must be cautious due to Serb anti-aircraft fire from the surrounding hills.

RIGHT:

Operation Deny Flight, Bosnia and Herzegovina

Staff Sergeant Jeffrey R. Seeley, a 53rd Fighter Squadron crew chief, talks with the pilot of their F-15C Eagle through an intercom system as the aircraft's engines fire for an Operation Deny Flight sortie to enforce the UN's established no-fly zone over Bosnia and Herzegovina. The aircraft is heavily armed with AIM-7 Sparrow missiles, AIM-120 advanced medium air-to-air missiles, and AIM-9 Sidewinder missiles.

LEFT:

The Phantom's last war, Saudi Arabia

A pair of 35th Tactical Fighter Wing F-4G Phantom II aircraft pass over the Saudi desert while on a training flight during Operation Desert Shield, the codename for the defense of Saudia Arabia against possible Iraqi invasion. The Phantoms are carrying external fuel tanks on their outboard wing pylons and AGM-88 high-speed anti-radiation missiles on the inboard wing pylons. The aircraft was retired from service by the USAF in 1996.

RIGHT:

Operation Desert Storm, Iraq

A USAF A-10A Thunderbolt II loitering over a target during Operation Desert Storm (the codename for the combat phase of the Gulf War, 1990–91), a war waged by coalition forces from 35 nations, led by the United States, against Iraq in response to Iraq's invasion and annexation of Kuwait. The A-10 saw combat for the first time during the Gulf War, destroying more than 900 Iraqi tanks, 2000 military vehicles, and 1200 artillery pieces.

Controlling the skies over Kuwait

Air Force F-16s, F-15Cs, and F-15Es of the 4th Tactical Fighter Wing (TFW) fly over burning Kuwaiti oil wells that were set ablaze by the retreating Iraqi army in 1991. The combat record of the 4th TFW in the Gulf War was exceptional, flying over 2200 combat missions. They lost two aircraft during the war; two pilots were killed in action and two were captured and released after the end of hostilities. The unit dropped more than 6 million lb (2.7 million kg) of bombs on Scud missile sites, bridges, and airfields; most of the missions were flown at night.

Training

The USAF's core missions are attaining and maintaining air and space superiority; conducting intelligence, surveillance, and reconnaissance; ensuring rapid global mobility; global strike capabilities; and ensuring command and control. As such, the 130-plus career specializations go toward the successful execution of these missions.

The training of Airmen starts with Basic Military Training (BMT), which introduces recruits to fundamental aspects of military service, such as physical and mental conditioning; the Air Force's rich heritage; its customs and courtesies; troop-leading skills; combat field exercises; rules of engagement; and responses to various types of chemical, biological, or nuclear attacks. After finishing BMT, enlisted Airmen head to technical schools to receive career-specific training. While enlisted Airmen can work their way up and attend Officer Training School, most officers either attend the Air Force Academy, join the Reserve Officer Training Corps in college, or enter Officer Training School after graduating college.

Airman participate in an array of job-specific training that simply cannot be adequately captured here. Likewise, training methods vary greatly from tabletop exercises to virtual-reality simulations to regular field training. The Air Force also helps plan annual large-scale, inter-service and international partner exercises, such as Red Flag, or take part in long-range Bomber Task Force training missions with NATO partner nations, providing aircrews with valuable, realistic training scenarios. Airmen opting for Special Warfare career paths that provide vital connections between air and ground operations require more extensive and strenuous training across an array of skillsets and may include temporary assignments to relevant units in other armed forces branches.

LEFT:
F-16 "Aggressors"
F-16 Fighting Falcons of the 18th Aggressor Squadron fly toward "blue forces" over the Joint Pacific Alaska Range Complex (all the land, air, sea, space, and cyberspace used for military training in Alaska). Air Force Aggressor squadron pilots are trained to use enemy tactics to provide the most realistic training situations possible for USAF pilots.

LEFT:

An Air Force base's first line of defense

Senior Airman Rosa Young, of the 891st Missile Security Forces Squadron, climbs an obstacle course net at Fort Harrison, Montana. Airmen are trained to adhere to the highest standards of personal reliability, dedication, and performance of duty. Security Forces personnel are an Air Force installation's first line of defense and are tasked with maintaining the rule of law on Air Force bases.

RIGHT:

Inter-Service Alpha Warrior Battle

USAF Senior Airman Stephanie Williams tackles the rings obstacle of the proving rig during the first Inter-Service Alpha Warrior Final Battle at Retama Park, Selma, Texas in 2018. The Air Force has won both Inter-Service Alpha Warrior competitions held to date.

Special operations training
Battlefield Airmen Preparatory
Course candidates participate
in pool exercises at Joint
Base San Antonio-Lackland,
Texas. Running, rucking, and
swimming are core areas of
Battlefield Airmen training.
These are units extensively
drilled for special operations
in land combat environments,
often going deep into hostile
territory, that help connect air
and ground operations.

TOP RIGHT:
Memorial training session
A special warfare trainee
from the 352nd Special
Warfare Training Squadron
participates in a memorial
physical training session at
the Triangle Pool, Keesler
Air Force Base, Mississippi.
The event was held for Staff
Sergeant Andrew Harvell, a
combat controller killed in
action in 2011.

BOTTOM RIGHT:
Tackling the assault course
The basic cadets of the US
Air Force Academy Class of
2023 test the assault course at
Jacks Valley training complex,
Colorado Springs, Colorado.
The course is physically and
mentally grueling, and puts
basic cadets through combat-
like situations during the final
phase of their training, with
the inclusion of simulated
small-arms fire, artillery
explosions, and obstacles.

ABOVE:

Air Force Search and rescue training

A pararescueman assigned to the 38th Rescue Squadron (from Moody Air Force Base, Georgia) fast-ropes from an HH-60G Pave Hawk in Eufaula, Alabama. The 38th and 41st Rescue Squadrons conduct water operations training, including tethered duck, which entails inserting a team of pararescuemen and a combat rubber raiding craft (CRRC) into the training arena, among other search and extraction methods.

RIGHT:

"Guardian Angels" polishing their skills, Afghanistan

A pararescueman of the 83rd Expeditionary Rescue Squadron, operates his parachute while conducting a high-altitude, high-opening military free-fall jump from a C-130J Super Hercules flown by the 774th Expeditionary Airlift Squadron (both units Bagram Airfield, Afghanistan). "Guardian Angel" teams train on all aspects of combat, medical, and search and rescue tactics to sharpen their skills and provide the highest level of tactical capabilities to combatant commanders.

LEFT:

Instructor pilot training
Pilots from the 39th Flying Training Squadron and 19th Air Force conduct instructor pilot training in a T-38C Talon. The 560th Flying Training Squadron qualifies pilots flying various airframes as instructor pilots in the T-38.

RIGHT:

"Hot-pit" refueling, Germany
A readiness and training flight chief drags a fuel hose to an F-16 Fighting Falcon during exercise Agile Wolf at Ramstein Air Base, Germany. The Agile Wolf exercise tested the ability of aircrews to perform "hot-pit" refueling during contingency operations.

TOP RIGHT:

Virtual reality training
Staff Sergeant Joseph Sabin of the Technology Integrated Detachment, Air Education and Training Command, flies a virtual-reality sortie at the Pilot Training Next Technology Expo.

BOTTOM RIGHT:

Repairing Army UH-60s
Airmen assigned to Detachment 1, 362nd Training Squadron, examine the engine of a UH-60 Black Hawk helicopter during a repairer course. Airmen will spend four months studying Black Hawks while also learning Army customs and courtesies so that they are able to work seamlessly with the Army units using the Black Hawks.

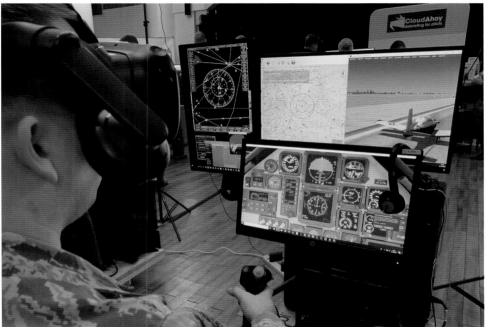

ABOVE LEFT:

Red Flag exercises

Staff Sergeant Vincent Yocco, a Joint Terminal Attack Controller assigned to the 116th Air Support Operations Squadron, during close air-support training at Red Flag-Alaska 19-2. This is an annual US Pacific Air Forces training exercise for US and international partners to develop and improve interoperability by planning and executing safe and effective joint and multilateral operations.

LEFT:

Training for chemical warfare scenarios

A Security Forces Airman with the 121st Air Refueling Wing participates in quarterly weapons training during a scheduled drill weekend at Rickenbacker Air National Guard Base, Ohio. Airmen used simulated ammunition to practice shooting while wearing gloves and gas masks to experience weapons handling in a chemical warfare situation.

ABOVE:

Pilot survival training, Italy

An non-commissioned officer in charge of survival, evasion, resistance, and escape training for the 31st Operations Support Squadron applies a bandage to the leg of Colonel Hauck, commander of the 31st Operations Group, to simulate a broken leg during a training exercise in Osoppo, Italy. Hauck acted as a downed pilot in need of rescue during Operation Porcupine, testing the diverse capabilities of the 31st Fighter Wing.

TACP training
Staff Sergeant Guillermo Pacheco, Battalion Tactical Air Control Party (TACP) NCO in charge, 3rd Air Support Operations Squadron (ASOS), evaluates Airman 1st Class Jared Best, 3rd ASOS TACP, as he sets up a ground-portable laser target designator. Pacheco organized the three-day field training to certify TACP Airmen as combat-mission ready.

LEFT:

Reserve pilots training to keep sharp

Captain Adam Stahl (left) and Major Jacob Predis, 758th Airlift Squadron pilots, perform preflight checks at the Pittsburgh International Airport Air Reserve Station, Pennsylvania. The flight provided vital training for aircrew members, which included practicing night-time touch-and-go landings at Wright-Patterson Air Force Base, Ohio.

RIGHT:

A B-1B aircrew with its European allies

A B-1B Lancer flies with a Danish F-16 during a training mission with Bomber Task Force Europe. Aircrews from the 28th Bomb Wing at Ellsworth Air Force Base, South Dakota, took off on the long-range, long-duration Bomber Task Force mission to perform interoperability training with NATO allies and partners. These operations illustrate and reinforce a shared commitment to global security and stability.

LEFT:

18th Aggressor Squadron

An F-16 Fighting Falcon of the 18th Aggressor Squadron during Red Flag-Alaska 11-1. Red Flag-Alaska is a series of Pacific Air Forces (the USAF major command that promotes US interests in the Asia-Pacific region during peacetime, through crisis, and in war) field exercises providing joint-offensive counter-air, interdiction, close-air support, and large-force-employment training in a simulated combat environment.

ABOVE:

Graduating basic training

Basic military training graduates from the 326th Training Squadron stand at attention during graduation, Joint Base San Antonio-Lackland, Texas, March 2020. Due to the Covid-19 pandemic, the 37th Training Wing implemented social distancing by graduating the 668 Airmen in four separate ceremonies at different training complexes. The ceremonies were closed to the public to protect the Airmen and their families.

Aircraft

The aircraft in the inventory of the United States Air Force are as diverse as the service's mission sets. Equally varied is the process of acquiring the aircraft. Some USAF planes are derivatives of existing commercial aircraft, such as with its mobility and executive airlift fleets. Others are designed from scratch, including fighters, bombers, and other high-performance and technologically advanced aircraft.

It is the mission of the Air Force Materiel Command (AFMC) to "develop, deliver, support, and sustain war-winning capabilities." Inside AFMC, it is the Air Force Life Cycle Management Center (AFLCMC) that guides the aircraft acquisition process through the key stages of the complex Defense Acquisition System outlined in the DoD 5000 series instructions. In doing so, AFLCMC collaborates with operational commands (Air Mobility Command, Air Combat Command, Air Force Global Strike Command, and the Air Force Special Operations Command), defense industry contractors, the Air Force Test Center, and the Air Force Sustainment Command to design, develop, test, produce, support, and maintain USAF aircraft from their inception to their retirement to the "boneyard" at Davis-Monthan Air Force Base, Arizona.

Two decades into the twenty-first century, and the USAF aircraft inventory is as old as it has ever been. For example, the B-52 Stratofortress was originally introduced into service in 1955; the C-130 Hercules, 1956; the KC-135 Stratotanker in 1957; and the U-2 Dragon Lady, 1957; the list of individual helicopters and aircraft that have been in continuous service since the 1960s and 1970s is long. While the Air Force has done a truly remarkable job of maintaining and modernizing these legacy planes with new systems, replacing them is among its top priorities.

LEFT:

F-22 Raptor refueling in-flight, Finland
An F-22 Raptor flies behind a KC-135 Stratotanker during aerial refueling training off the coast of Finland. The F-22 deployed from the 27th Fighter Squadron, Joint Base Langley–Eustis, Virginia. The Air Force will be replacing its venerable KC-135 fleet with the new KC-46 Pegasus tankers.

LEFT:

F-22 Raptor, England

An F-22 Raptor from the 1st Fighter Wing, Joint Base Langley–Eustis, takes off at RAF Lakenheath, England. The Air Force has deployed F-22s, Airmen, and associated equipment to RAF Lakenheath for a flying training deployment to conduct air training with other Europe-based US aircraft and NATO allies.

RIGHT:

F-15C Eagle, Operation Iraqi Freedom

An F-15C Eagle turns away from a tanker aircraft after receiving a full fuel load high above the deserts of Southwest Asia. The F-15 is a part of the 33rd Fighter Wing, Eglin Air Force Base, Florida. The F-15 is a Mach 2-class tactical fighter that has been in continuous service since 1974.

OVERLEAF:

F-16s of the 52nd Fighter Wing, Germany

F-16 Fighting Falcons from the 52nd Fighter Wing line up in formation on the runway for a show-of-force display at Spangdahlem Air Base, Germany. The 52nd Fighter Wing provides the only suppression of enemy air defenses squadron (the 480th Fighting Squadron) in the USAF in Europe.

LEFT:

F-35A Lightning II Joint Strike Fighter

Captain Kristin Wolfe, F-35A Lightning II Demonstration Team pilot, performs the "dedication pass" maneuver during practice at Hill Air Force Base, Utah. The maneuver is intended to give an aerial salute to service members past and present. The multirole F-35A variant is intended to replace the F-16 and A-10 Thunderbolt II fleets.

RIGHT:

A-10 Thunderbolt II

An A-10 Thunderbolt II from the 355th Fighter Squadron at Eielson Air Force Base, Alaska, fires its 30mm GAU-8 Avenger seven-barrel Gatling gun at the Pacific Alaska Range Complex. "BRRRRRTTTT" is the sound its GAU-8 makes when fired—a popular hashtag often found in discussions of the A-10 on social media. As an effective close air support aircraft, the A-10 is beloved by American ground troops.

153

B-1B Lancer

Carrying the largest payload of conventional guided and unguided weapons in the Air Force inventory, the multi-mission B-1B is the foundation of the USAF's long-range bomber force. Together, its variable-wing configuration and turbofan afterburning engines provide long range, maneuverability, high speed, and enhanced survivability.

B-1B preparing for takeoff

A USAF B-1B Lancer aircraft starts its engine during exercise Red Flag-Alaska 07-1. Red Flag-Alaska is a field training exercise for US forces flown under simulated air combat conditions conducted on the Pacific Alaskan Range Complex with air operations flown out of Eielson and Elmendorf Air Force Bases.

B-52G Stratofortress, Operation Desert Storm
A B-52G Stratofortress bomber aircraft of the 1708th Bomb Wing takes off on a mission during Operation Desert Storm in 1991. The latest model, the B-52H, continues the aircraft's heavy bomber mission, delivering either nuclear or precision-guided conventional munitions, and boasts global precision navigation capability. For more than 60 years, it has been at the center of the Air Force's strategic-bombing mission.

LEFT:
**E-3A Sentry (AWACS),
Operation Northern Watch**
A USAF E-3A Sentry Airborne
Warning and Control System
(AWACS) aircraft assigned
to the 970th Expeditionary
Aerospace Air Control
Squadron (EAACS) lands
at Incirlik Air Base, Turkey,
after completing a mission
in support of Operation
Northern Watch, which
enforced a no-fly zone over
Iraq from 1997 to 2003.

RIGHT:
B-2 Spirit
The B-2 Spirit multirole
stealth bomber is the newest
bomber in the USAF fleet,
introduced into service in
December 1993. Its "stealth"
characteristics give it the
unique ability to penetrate
the most sophisticated
defenses and threaten valued,
heavily defended targets.
This capability provides
strong, effective deterrence
across the globe.

E-4B National Airborne Operations Center

An E-4B National Airborne Operations Center, first delivered in January 1980, taxis around the tarmac for takeoff from Offutt Air Force Base, Nebraska. The E-4B provides travel support for the Secretary of Defense and staff to ensure command and control connectivity outside of the continental United States. It is a militarized version of the Boeing 747-200 commercial airliner.

E-11A, Afghanistan
A 430th Expeditionary Electronic Combat Squadron (EECS) E-11A aircraft outfitted with a Battlefield Airborne Communications Node (BACN) sits on the runway at Kandahar Airfield, Afghanistan. The 430th EECS is the only unit that operates with the BACN real-time information system.

AC-130U Spooky Gunship
An AC-130U Spooky Gunship from the 4th Special Operations Squadron jettisons flares over an area near Hurlburt Field, Florida. The flares are used as a countermeasure to heat-seeking missiles that can track aircraft during missions. The AC-130 provides close air support of ground forces and interdiction missions against pre-determined targets or targets of opportunity.

ABOVE:
C-130 Hercules
A C-130 Hercules from the Nevada Air National Guard's 152nd Airlift Wing conducts flight operations. The C-130 Hercules has been a workhorse for the USAF for more than 60 years. Designed to transport troops and equipment into combat zones, variants of the C-130 operate throughout the Air Force, fulfilling a wide range of operational missions in the Air Mobility Command, Air Force Special Operations Command, Air Combat Command, US Air Forces in Europe and Air Forces Africa, Pacific Air Forces, Air National Guard, and Air Force Reserve Command.

RIGHT:
C-5A Galaxy
People line up to get a look inside the 445th Airlift Wing's first C-5A Galaxy at Wright-Patterson Air Force Base in 2005. The massive C-5 cargo transport replaced the retiring C-141 Starlifter and entered service in 1970. The latest model, the C-5M Super Galaxy, introduced in 2006, was re-engined and upgraded with advanced avionics, and will be in service through 2040. The 445th Airlift Wing transitioned from the C-5 to the C-17 Globemaster III in 2012.

ABOVE:

HH-60G Pave Hawk

An HH-60G Pave Hawk helicopter maneuvers into position to refuel from an HC-130P/N King over the Arizona desert. The Pave Hawk is assigned to the 55th Rescue Squadron and the King to the 79th Rescue Squadron. The primary mission of the HH-60G is performing isolated personnel recovery operations in hostile environments during war. It is scheduled to be replaced by the HH-60W Jolly Green II.

RIGHT:

"Iron Horse" HC-130P King

HC-130P #62-1863, nicknamed "Iron Horse," readies for departure. Over the course of its career, "Iron Horse" has flown for over 27,000 hours, performing multiple missions starting in the Vietnam War. The HC-130P and HC-130N King are the only dedicated fixed-wing personnel recovery platforms in the Air Force fleet. It can rapidly deploy to austere airfields and denied territory to undertake all-weather personnel recovery operations, day or night.

A C-17 Globemaster III repatriates Americans
A US Air Force C-17 Globemaster III aircraft carrying three former hostages arrives on Lackland Air Force Base, Texas in July 2008. The defense contract employees were rescued by Colombian forces, having spent more than five years in the captivity of Colombian guerilla fighters after their plane crashed in the jungle. The C-17 is the most flexible cargo aircraft in the USAF airlift force and is capable of rapid delivery of troops and cargo to main operating bases or forward bases in the deployment area. It has also transported ambulatory patients during aeromedical evacuations.

KC-10, Afghanistan

An F/A-18C from the "Knighthawks" of Strike Fighter Squadron 136 (VFA-136) receives fuel from an Air Force KC-10 during a close-air support mission over Afghanistan in 2006. The VFA-136 is deployed aboard the nuclear-powered aircraft carrier USS *Enterprise*, supporting the Global War on Terror.

A KC-10 boom operator refueling an F-15, Operation Iraqi Freedom

Master Sergeant Todd McPeak refuels an F-15E Strike Eagle during an Operation Iraqi Freedom mission. He is a boom operator aboard a KC-10 Extender with the 908th Expeditionary Air Refueling Squadron. The KC-10 has been in service since 1981. At present, the Extender fleet numbers 58, with the first retirement occurring in July 2020. Planes are retired when they reach a threshold of flight hours, rather than an aircraft's age, as this is a better determinant for safety.

KC-46 Pegasus
A KC-46 Pegasus refuels an
A-10 Thunderbolt II with
1500lb (680kg) of fuel. This
mission was the last of the
flight tests required for the
Undersecretary of Defense
for Acquisition, Technology,
and Logistics to approve
the KC-46 to enter into
initial production (known as
"Milestone C" in the Defense
Acquisition System). This
approval was received in
August 2016.

The boom operator's view aboard a KC-135
A boom operator aboard a refueling tanker is the aircrew member responsible for transferring fuel from the tanker to the aircraft being refueled in-flight. The "boom" is the long metal arm that is attached to the rear underside of the tanker and extends to the fuel receptacle of the aircraft receiving the fuel.

KC-135 Stratotanker refueling F-22 Raptors
A KC-135 Stratotanker from the 101st Air Refueling Wing refuels F-22 Raptors from the 94th Fighter Squadron over the Atlantic Ocean. The 94th is the second oldest fighter squadron in the USAF; the oldest is the 27th, and both it and the 94th are F-22 units stationed at Joint Base Langley–Eustis, Virginia.

LEFT:

UV-18B Twin Otter
A US Air Force UV-18B Twin Otter carries the "Wings of Blue" skydiving demonstration team during the "Thunder and Lightning over Arizona" Open House at Davis–Monthan Air Force Base, Arizona in 2016. The team travels across the country to airshows, sporting events, and other venues to represent the Air Force in precision parachuting.

BELOW LEFT:

Special Operations C-145A and C-146A on the runway
A C-145A Skytruck (foreground) and a C-146A Wolfhound (background) sit on the flightline at Duke Field, Florida, waiting for their next mission. The two planes are the primary aircraft of the 919th Special Operations Wing.

RIGHT:

E-9A Widget
An E-9A Widget assigned to the 82nd Aerial Targets Squadron, Tyndall Air Force Base, Florida, takes flight on a Combat Archer—the Air Force's air-to-air Weapons System Evaluation Program—mission. The E-9 uses radar to track the trajectory of missiles and transmits the data to the range safety officer to calculate the target area for weapons tests.

LEFT:

U-28A: the Jack of all trades

A USAF U-28A sits under a sunshade on the flightline at Hurlburt Field, Florida. The U-28A is certified to operate from short and semi-prepared airfields and provides manned, fixed-wing tactical airborne intelligence, surveillance, and reconnaissance (ISR) support, humanitarian operations, search and rescue missions, and conventional and special operation missions. It is nothing if not versatile.

ABOVE:

E-8C JSTAR

An Electronic Systems Center team working with an E-8C Joint Surveillance Target Attack Radar (JSTAR) system has been participating in the Joint Surface Warfare Joint Capability Technology Demonstration. The E-8C JSTAR is an airborne battle management, command and control, ISR aircraft that provides ground and air commanders with surveillance and targeting to support attack operations against enemy forces.

A U-2 departs on a surveillance mission, Afghanistan

A U-2 Dragon Lady of the 380th Air Expeditionary Wing, stationed at Al Dhafra Air Base, United Arab Emirates, takes off from Bagram Airfield, Afghanistan. To make up for the pilot's limited movement and vision inside the aircraft, mobile chase-car drivers act as a second pair of eyes and ears for U-2 pilots during takeoff and landing. Once an aircraft nears the runway, chase cars speed off in pursuit close behind it, radioing adjustments to the pilot until they are inches from the ground.

U-2 Dragon Lady
A U-2 Dragon Lady flies above the Sierra Nevada mountain range, California. The U-2 is a single-seat, single-engine, high-altitude/near-space ISR aircraft that delivers critical imagery and signals intelligence to decision makers in all phases of conflict. This includes peacetime signals and warnings, low-intensity conflict, and large-scale hostilities.

WC-135W Constant Phoenix
The WC-135W Constant Phoenix is a special-purpose aircraft derived from the Boeing C-135 Stratolifter. Its mission is as an atmospheric sampling aircraft, collecting particulates and gaseous emissions and debris from accessible regions of the atmosphere to detect nuclear incidents in support of the Limited Nuclear Test Ban Treaty of 1963.

LEFT:
RQ-4B Global Hawk, Japan
The USAF RQ-4B Global Hawk unmanned surveillance aircraft on display in Aomori, Japan. The RQ-4 is a high-altitude, long-endurance, remotely piloted aircraft with an integrated sensor suite that provides global all-weather, near-real-time ISR capabilities day or night.

ABOVE:
WC-130J Hercules
A WC-130J Hercules from 53rd Weather Reconnaissance Squadron takes off in support of Operation Surge Capacity. Sixteen aircraft from the 403rd Wing took part in the exercise. The "Hurricane Hunter" is a C-130J transport configured with palletized weather instrumentation for penetration of tropical disturbances, tropical storms, hurricanes, and winter storms to obtain data on their movement, size, and intensity.

ABOVE:
C-37B
An 89th Airlift Wing C-37B is parked on the ramp before flight. The 89th is the only unit in the Air Force to operate this aircraft. The twin-engine plane transports high-ranking government and Department of Defense officials, and features enhanced weather capabilities, a modern heads-up display for the pilot, and secure voice and data communications equipment.

RIGHT:
EC-130H Compass Call
The EC-130H is an electronic attack aircraft based on the C-130 Hercules that can quickly be deployed worldwide to support tactical air, surface, and special operations forces. It has been upgraded to jam enemy command and control communications, as well as undertake offensive counterinformation missions. It will also be upgraded to attack enemy early-warning systems.

T-6 Texan II
These T-6A Texan IIs are single-engine, two-seat primary trainers designed to educate Joint Primary Pilot Training (JPPT) students in basic flying skills common to US Air Force and Navy pilots. Instructor pilot training in the T-6A began at Randolph Air Force Base, Texas in 2000 and JPPT in 2001 at Moody Air Force Base, Georgia.

T-38A Talon
A USAF 25th Flying Training Squadron instructor pilot and his student walk toward their Northrop T-38A Talon to begin flight training. The design, ease of maintenance and operation, high performance, and exceptional safety record make the twin-engine, high-altitude, supersonic jet an excellent undergraduate pilot trainer.

T-53A

The T-53A fleet is the mainstay of the USAF Academy's Powered Flight training program, in which more than 500 cadets participate annually. The 306th Flying Training Group is assigned to the Academy as their instructors.

TG-15A

Air Force Academy cadets also fly TG-15A gliders. The students typically fly 10 to 15 training sorties in the TG-15A and undergo 50-hour cross-country training before they can advance to flying cross-country solo in a TG-15B glider.

MQ-9 Reaper
A remotely piloted MQ-9 Reaper flies over the Nevada Test and Training Range. MQ-9 aircrew provide dominant, persistent attack and reconnaissance capabilities for combatant commanders and coalition partners around the world. The MQ-9 is larger and more heavily armed than its predecessor, the MQ-1 Predator, and attacks time-sensitive targets repeatedly and precisely to destroy or disable them.

RQ-11 Raven, Iraq
Senior Airman Glenn Gerald, a 506th Expeditionary Security Forces Squadron Raven operator, prepares to put an RQ-11 Raven into flight during a mission at Kirkuk Air Base, Iraq. Weighing in at less than 5lb (2.27kg), these small unmanned aerial vehicles are critical to securing the installation and surrounding neighborhoods.

LEFT:

EQ-4 Global Hawk
US Airmen assigned to
the 380th Expeditionary
Aircraft Maintenance
Squadron recover an EQ-4
Global Hawk unmanned
aircraft at an undisclosed
location in Southwest Asia.
Called the "Workhorse" by
its maintainers, the EQ-4
completed its 500th sortie
on Veterans Day 2015.

ABOVE:

**Space-Based Infrared System
on the Atlas V rocket**
An Atlas V rocket carrying
the Space-Based Infrared
System (SBIRS) GEO
Flight 4 satellite launched
from Cape Canaveral in
January 2018. The SBIRS
delivers missile warning and
infrared surveillance data to
combatant commanders and
authorized officials.

ABOVE RIGHT:

Missileers at work
First Lieutenant Daniel
Cook, missile combat
crew commander, and 2nd
Lieutenant Kyle Todd,
deputy missile combat crew
commander, both of the 319th
Missile Squadron, man the
launch control center of the
Delta-01 missile alert facility
at F.E. Warren Air Force Base,
Wyoming.

TH-1H Huey
Captain John Beurer (right) pilots a TH-1H Huey trainer helicopter with instructor pilot Jeff Cutrell. This is the first of 24 TH-1Hs that will be modified to train student helicopter pilots. Some of the helicopter modifications include an engine upgrade from 1400 to 1600 brake horsepower; a stronger transmission, main rotor shaft, and tail boom; a repositioned tail rotor to the right side for better efficiency; an all-new "glass cockpit" with three large, multi-function displays; and an emergency location transmitter.

LEFT:

Unloading an HH-60G Pave Hawk

Aircrew prepare to unload an HH-60G Pave Hawk helicopter assigned to the 305th Rescue Squadron from a C-5M Super Galaxy cargo aircraft of the 512th Airlift Wing at MacDill Air Force Base, Florida in order to take part in a joint exercise. The HH-60 is a derivative of the UH-60 Black Hawk and is used for the recovery of personnel under hostile conditions.

ABOVE:

The "fini flight"

Airmen assigned to the 347th Rescue Group (RQG) drop flares from an HH-60G Pave Hawk during a "fini flight" for Colonel Bryan Creel, 347th RQG commander at Moody Air Force Base, Georgia. The fini flight is a long-standing Air Force tradition that occurs when a pilot departs from an assigned unit.

HH-60G Pave Hawk, Italy
An HH-60G Pave Hawk
helicopter operated by the
56th Rescue Squadron (RQS)
flies over Aviano Air Base,
Italy. The 56th RQS integrates
with the Guardian Angel
weapons system and other
special forces to support the
insertion, extraction, and
recovery of US and allied
combatants.

UH-1N Huey, Japan
Technical Sergeant Michael
Wright, a 459th Airlift
Squadron special mission
aviator evaluator, holds onto
the cable as Master Sergeant
Antonio Gueits, a 374th
Operation Group resource
adviser, is hoisted up into a
UH-1N Huey from a drop
zone near Mount Fuji, Japan.

LEFT:
CV-22B Osprey
Air commandos with the 801st Special Operations Aircraft Maintenance Squadron (SOAMXS) accept delivery of a new CV-22B Osprey tiltrotor aircraft. The 801st SOAMXS keeps Ospreys ready to execute infiltration, exfiltration, and resupply missions worldwide. The CV-22 can take off, hover, and land vertically, but flies like a turboprop aircraft.

ABOVE:
CV-22 weapons system practice, England
An air commando from the 7th Special Operations Squadron fires a .50-caliber machine gun aboard a CV-22 Osprey during a flight around southern England. The Osprey flew to a range where the crew sighted, loaded, and ran through technical and tactical procedures to re-qualify on the .50-caliber weapons system. This is the only armament on the CV-22.

21st Century Conflicts

In the twenty-first century, the Air Force has continued to spearhead American military operations, just as it had in Southeast Asia during the Gulf War and in Operation Allied Force in the Balkans.

In October 2001, Operation Enduring Freedom began with air strikes on Taliban targets in Afghanistan. These were carried out by B-2 stealth bombers flying from Missouri—the longest bombing missions in the history of military aviation—as well as B-1B Lancers and B-52 Stratofortresses. As Taliban and al Qaeda fighters retreated eastward, the American-led coalition commenced Operation Anaconda, where USAF B-52 and B-1 bombers, AC-130 gunships, A-10 Thunderbolt IIs and F-15E Strike Eagles pummeled the cave system in which the fighters were hiding.

In the March 2003 invasion of Iraq, it was Air Force stealth F-117 Nighthawks that dropped GBU-27 laser-guided bombs on high-value targets southwest of Baghdad, commencing Operation Iraqi Freedom. In its first six weeks, coalition air forces flew more than 41,000 sorties, with the USAF accounting for more than half of that total; Air Force C-130s and C-17s dropped coalition paratroops and transported over 12,000 tons (11,000 tonnes) of materiel; Air Force tankers flew more than 6000 missions, distributing more than 376 million lb (171 million kg) of fuel to coalition aircraft. The USAF has continued to support US operations in both Afghanistan and Iraq since the beginning of those campaigns.

The USAF continues to play a leading role in combatting Islamic State fighters in Iraq, Syria, and Libya as a part of Operation Inherent Resolve. As Generals Arnold and Spaatz had envisioned, the Air Force has remained on the cutting edge of technology and is poised to remain at the forefront of US military operations in the twenty-first century.

LEFT:
MQ-9 Reaper ready for combat, Afghanistan
An armed MQ-9 Reaper unmanned aerial vehicle (UAV) taxis down a runway in Afghanistan. With its ability to loiter above potential targets, its wide-ranging sensors, advanced communications suite, and precision-guided weapons (such as a 500lb (227kg) GBU-12 munition), the MQ-9 gives the Air Force a unique capacity to perform strike missions against highly valued, transitory targets.

LEFT:

Explosive Ordnance Disposal, Afghanistan
Staff Sergeant Greg Talley, assigned to the 755th Air Expeditionary Group, searches for and dismantles explosive devices before they can harm anyone. Explosive Ordinance Disposal (EOD) technicians have one of the most dangerous jobs in the Air Force: beyond losing 20 EOD technicians in the last two wars, roughly 150 more EOD techs sustained serious injuries.

ABOVE:

F-22 on a sortie, Iraq
A USAF F-22 Raptor on its way to meet a KC-135 Stratotanker assigned to the 28th Expeditionary Air Refueling Squadron at Al Udeid Air Base, Qatar, for an in-flight refuel mission over Iraq in support of Operation Inherent Resolve. The multirole F-22 represents an exponential leap in capabilities, combining stealth, sustained supersonic flight (supercruise), advanced maneuverability, integrated avionics, and is designed to be easier to maintain.

RIGHT:

PJs conducting a rescue training mission, Afghanistan
An HH-60G Pave Hawk hovers over pararescuemen of the 33rd Rescue Squadron and Brigadier General Jack L. Briggs (center), the 455th Air Expeditionary Wing commander, during a training mission at Bagram Airfield, Afghanistan. Pararescuemen, known alternatively by their duty identifier, "PJ," are among the most highly trained special operations forces in the US military.

LEFT:

Unloading valuable cargo, Afghanistan

A C-17 Globemaster III loadmaster helps the driver of a mine-resistant, ambush-protected all-terrain vehicle (M-ATV) offload the vehicle at Bagram Airfield, Afghanistan. The M-ATVs were the first in Afghanistan and supported small-unit combat operations in hazardous and contested rural, mountainous, and urban environments. The USAF Air Mobility Command can airlift them in a day, rather than in nearly a month by sea.

ABOVE:

Airdropping vital supplies to ground troops, Afghanistan

Staff Sergeant Christopher Bankston, a loadmaster in the 816th Expeditionary Airlift Squadron, watches as fuel and other supplies are dropped from a C-17 Globemaster III over a remote forward operating base in Afghanistan. Air Force airlift squadrons have been providing an essential lifeline to US and allied ground troops since 1942 and the establishment of the Air Transport Command.

LEFT:

Pararescuemen landing during a medical evacuation exercise, Afghanistan

An Air Force HH-60G Pave Hawk helicopter carrying combat search and rescue airmen approaches the landing zone during a 2010 exercise at Bagram Airfield, Afghanistan. The exercise tested the rescue squadron's ability to treat and evacuate the wounded in an austere location while under simulated fire. If Air Force PJs can evacuate a wounded soldier to a theater hospital, their chance of survival increases exponentially.

ABOVE:

Air Force Security Forces on patrol, Iraq

Staff Sergeant Benjamin Wilson, of the 532nd Expeditionary Security Forces Squadron (ESFS), patrols a village on the outskirts of Joint Base Balad, Iraq in April 2010. The 532nd ESFS was tasked with screening entry into the base, patrolling the surrounding area to disrupt and deter indirect fire attacks and the placement of IEDs along transportation routes, as well as to provide tactical security for Air Force Office of Special Investigations operations.

LEFT:

F-16s on a sortie, Iraq
An F-16 Fighting Falcon
launches electronic
countermeasure flares
following an aerial refueling
mission. The F-16 is a
compact, multirole fighter. It
is highly maneuverable and a
proven air-to-air combat and
air-to-surface attack aircraft.
Its relatively low cost and
high performance have made
the F-16 an asset to the USAF
since 1979.

TOP RIGHT:

Armored A-10, Afghanistan
The rugged A-10 "Warthog"
is equipped with a titanium-
armored cockpit and
reinforced primary structural
sections that enable it to
survive direct hits from
armor-piercing and high-
explosive projectiles of up to
0.9in/23mm.

BELOW RIGHT:

F-15E, Afghanistan
An F-15E Strike Eagle deploys
electronic countermeasure
flares during a mission.
The F-15E's primary role
in Afghanistan has been to
provide close-air support
to US ground troops.

FAR RIGHT:

**Airdropping supplies,
Afghanistan**
Delivery system bundles
containing food and water fall
from an 816th Expeditionary
Airlift Squadron C-17
Globemaster III onto a drop
zone during a high-altitude
airdrop mission.

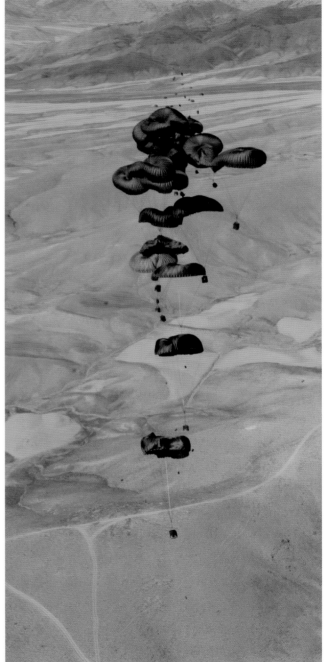

TOP LEFT:

Evacuating an injured Iraqi soldier, Iraq

US and Iraqi airmen load an Iraqi servicemember wounded in combat into an Iraqi Air Force Mi-17 Hip helicopter at Joint Base Balad, Iraq. The USAF has been assisting the Iraqi Air Force in re-establishing its aeromedical evacuation service.

LEFT:

Pararescuemen training, Iraq

A pararescueman assigned to the 64th Expeditionary Rescue Squadron, stationed at Joint Base Balad, fast-ropes from an HH-60 Pave Hawk helicopter during a proficiency exercise outside of Baghdad.

ABOVE:

USAF air traffic controllers at work, Iraq

USAF Airmen bring aircraft into Joint Base Balad as a C-17 Globemaster III from McCord Air Force Base, Washington taxis past the air traffic control tower. Balad Air Base controls over 200,000 square miles (518,000 sq km) of air space over Iraq and is the busiest single-runway airfield managed by the Department of Defense and is the second busiest in the world.

RIGHT:

The versatility of the F-35

Two Air Force F-35 Lightning IIs fly over the US Central Command (USCENTCOM) region of responsibility, which takes in Egypt and all of western Asia up to the borders of India and China. The supersonic, multirole, stealth F-35 is a major advancement in the mission to achieve air dominance, with enhanced lethality and survivability in hostile airspaces. It was designed to bring new flexibility and a range of abilities to the USAF and its allies. Missions previously requiring different, specialized aircraft can be executed by a squadron of F-35s.

LEFT:

An F-35 deploying a Peregrine missile

An F-35 Lightning II pilot deploys a Peregrine missile from the aircraft's internal bomb bay. On 30 April 2019, two Air Force F-35A Lightning II fighters conducted an air strike with a Joint Direct Attack Munitions (JDAMs) to destroy an ISIS tunnel network and weapons cache deep in the Hamrin Mountains, Wadi Ashai, Iraq. The attack, part of Operation Inherent Resolve, marked the very first combat engagement of F-35 Joint Strike Fighters.

RIGHT:

F-15s in Operation Inherent Resolve, Iraq

An F-15E Strike Eagle fires electronic countermeasure flares during an Operation Inherent Resolve mission, Iraq in 2017. F-15Es flew a significant portion of the USAF sorties against ISIS, including the air strikes on Islamic State leaders and camps in Libya. While the F-15 was designed as an air dominance fighter, the Strike Eagle was developed to assume a ground strike role.

F-15 Eagles on Icelandic Air Policing

Three F-15C/D Eagles assigned to the 493rd Expeditionary Fighter Squadron conduct a routine aerial mission in support of NATO operations from Keflavik Air Base, Iceland, October 2020. Operations like the NATO Air Police mission are designed to provide a collective defense for all allied countries in the Arctic sphere.

Picture Credits

Airsealand.Photos: 29, 31, 33 top and bottom right, 39 left, 40–43 all, 50, 58, 60 left, 61–71 all , 73, 75 left, 76, 77, 79–84 all, 86–90 all, 95–99 all, 101–104 all, 108–113 all, 114 right–119 all, 123

Alamy: 85 (Glasshouse Images)

Danish Air Force: 143

Getty Images: 56 (Hulton Archive/Fox Photos/M McNeill), 124 (Leif Skoogfors/Corbis), 125 (USAF)

Library of Congress: 26, 33 left, 36 left, 37, 39 right, 75 right

National Archives & Records Administration: 32, 34, 54, 74, 105, 114 left

National Museum of the U.S. Air Force: 24, 27, 28, 30, 35, 38, 45–49 all, 51–53 all, 57, 60 right, 63, 72, 78, 91, 94, 100

Shutterstock: 186 (Viper-zero)

Swedish Armed Forces: 11 top

U.S. Air Force: 6 (R Nial Baradshaw), 8 (TSgt Robert Cloys), 9 (TSgt Erik Cardenas), 10 (TSgt Emerson Nuñez), 11 bottom (SrA River Bruce), 12/13 (A1C Christina Bennett), 14 (Joshua J Seybert), 15 left (SSgt Tabitha Kuykendall), 15 top right (TSgt Sabrina Johnson), 15 bottom right (SSgt Joshua Kleinholz), 16 top left (A1C Taylor D Slater), 16 bottom left (SrA Jacqueline Romero), 16 right (SSgt Patrick Evenson), 17 (TSgt Joseph Swafford), 18 (SrA Kevin Tanenbaum), 19 left (Giancarlo Casem), 19 right (TSgt Lionel Castellano), 20 (SrA Racheal E Watson), 21 (Yasuo Osakabe), 22 (SrA Malcolm Mayfield), 23 (SrA Maeson L Elleman), 92 (Brian Shul), 106/107 (TSgt Frank Garzelnick), 120 (Ken Hackman), 121 (Judson Brohmer), 122 (MSgt Ken Hammond), 127 (TSgt Fernando Serna), 128/129, 130 (SSgt Christopher Boitz), 132 (A1C Tristan Truesdell), 133 (Debbie Aragon), 134 (Ismael Ortega), 135 top (Kemberly Groue), 135 bottom (Trevor Cokley), 136 (A1C Taryn Butler), 137 (TSgt Gregory Brook), 138 (MSgt Christopher Boitz), 139 left (A1C Alison Stewart), 139 top right (Dan Hawkins), 139 bottom right (A1C Monica Roybal), 140 top left (A1C Taylor Phifer), 140 right (TSgt Tory Cusimano), 141 (Capt Kay Magdalena Nissen), 142 (Joshua J Seybert), 144 (SSgt Christopher Boitz), 146 (SrA Luke Milano), 148 (SrA Malcolm Mayfield), 149 (MSgt Mark Bucher), 150/151 (SSgt Joshua R M Dewberry), 152 (Capt Kip Sumner), 153 (A1C Jonathan Snyder), 154 (MSgt Lance Cheung), 155 (A1C Jonathan Snyder), 156/157 (SrA Chris Putnam), 158 (SSgt Jason W Gamble), 159 (SSgt Cherie A Thurlby), 160/161 (SSgt Jacob Skovo), 162/163 (Capt Anna-Marie Wyant), 164/165 (SrA Julianne Showalter), 166 (Heide Couch), 167 (TSgt Charlie Miller), 168 (A1C Veronica Pierce), 169 (A1C Dillian Bamman), 170/171 (MSgt Lance Cheung), 173 (SrA Brian Ferguson), 174/175 (John D Parker/Boeing), 176 (SSgt Travis Aston), 177 (TSgt Natasha Stannard), 178 top (SrA Chris Massey), 178 bottom (TSgt Sam King), 179 (MSgt Michael Ammons), 180 (SSgt John Bainter), 181, 182/183 (SSgt Kristin High), 184 (SSgt Robert M Trujillo), 185 (Josh Plueger), 187 (TSgt Ryan Labadens), 188 (SSgt Kenny Holston), 189 (Maj Dale Greer), 190 (TSgt Jeffrey Allen), 191 (Terry Wasson), 193 (TSgt Samuel Bendet), 194/195 (A1C William Rio Rosado), 196 & 197 (SMSgt Don Senger), 198 (TSgt Frank Miller), 199 left (A1C Dalton Williams), 199 right (A1C Jason Wiese), 200/201 (MSgt Lance Cheung), 202 (A1C Ryan C Grossklag), 203 (SrA Hayden Legg), 204 (AB Thomas S Keisler IV), 205 (SSgt David Owsianka), 206 (A1C Nathan LeVang), 207 (SSgt Philip Steiner), 208 (SSgt Brian Ferguson), 210 left (TSgt John Jung), 210 right (SrA Xavier Navarro), 211 (SSgt Christopher Boitz), 212 (SrA Susan Tracy), 213 (MSgt Adrian Cadiz), 214 (SSgt Christopher Boitz), 215 (SSgt Quinton Russ), 217 both left (SSgt Aaron Allmon), 217 right (SSgt James L Harper Jr), 218 top left (A1C Jason Epley), 218 bottom left (SSgt James L Harper Jr), 218 right (SrA Brian Ferguson), 219 (A1C Duncan C Bevan), 220 (MSgt Michael Jackson), 221 (SSgt Trevor T McBride), 222/223 (MSgt Matthew Plew)

U.S. Air National Guard: 140 bottom left (SSgt Wendy Kuhn)

U.S. Department of Defense: 126, 145 (Johnny Saldivar), 216

U.S. Navy: 172 (Lt Peter Scheu)

Wikimedia Commons: 192